CHARLES HODGE'S CRITIQUE OF DARWINISM

An Historical-Critical Analysis of Concepts Basic to the 19th Century Debate

Jonathan Wells

Studies in American Religion
Volume 27

The Edwin Mellen Press
Lewiston/Queenston

Library of Congress Cataloging-in-Publication Data

Wells, Jonathan.
    Charles Hodges critique of Darwinism: an historical-critical
analysis of concepts basic to the 19th century debate / Jonathan
Wells.
        p. cm. -- (Studies in American religion ; v. 27)
    Bibliography: p.
    Includes index.
    ISBN 0-88946-671-8
    1. Evolution--Religious aspects--Christianity--History of
doctrines--19th century. 2. Hodge, Charles, 1797-1878--Views of
Darwin's theory of evolution. 3. Darwin, Charles, 1809-1882.
I. Title. II. Series.
BT712.W45 1988   87-31222
231.7'65--dc19   CIP

This is volume 27 in the continuing series
Studies in American Religion
Volume 27 ISBN 0-88946-671-8
SAR Series ISBN 0-88946-992-X

The Edwin Mellen Press   The Edwin Mellen Press
Box 450   Box 67
Lewiston, New York   Queenston, Ontario
USA 14092   L0S 1L0 CANADA

Printed in the United States of America

TABLE OF CONTENTS

FOREWORD

This study grew out of my long-standing interest in the relationship between Darwinian evolution and Christian theology. Since many accounts of this relationship seem to me to be superficial, confused, or even mistaken, I set out to clarify some of the major issues. I did not originally plan to study Charles Hodge, but in the course of my research it became clear that Hodge's critique of Darwinism dealt with precisely those issues which interest me most. It also became clear to me that Hodge has been misrepresented and unfairly criticized by some historians. My primary objective is thus to clarify some significant theological issues in the Darwinian controversies, and my secondary objective is to correct some common misperceptions of Hodge's position in those controversies.

In order to prevent misunderstanding, I would like to state at the outset that I am not a biblical fundamentalist or scientific creationist. I am persuaded that evolution -- by which I mean the derivation over very long periods of time of new species from previously existing ones -- is a fact. On the other hand, I am not a Darwinian. I am persuaded that Darwinism -- by which I mean Darwin's theory of the natural selection of accidental variations -- is inadequate as an explanation of the causes of evolution. The present study, however, is not concerned with the adequacy or truth of either Christianity or Darwinism, but only with with the nature of the conceptual conflict between them.

Some preliminary comments about scholarly apparatus are in order. So much has been written about the Darwinian controversies that any new study of them must take into account scores of secondary works in addition to the many primary sources. In order to focus attention on the latter, and to improve readability, I have chosen not to cite the authors of secondary works by name in the text of this essay. Where relevant, of course, they are cited by name in the notes; but the text is, I hope, somewhat less cluttered than it would have been had I included in it explicit references to secondary as well as primary authors. For the same reasons, I have tried to minimize the number of notes by combining, wherever possible, several sources in one note. In such cases, the sources are listed in the note in the order in which they are quoted in the text; supplementary material in the same note is referred to by "See also...", and is listed in alphabetical order, to distinguish it from material actually quoted.

I am indebted to David Kelsey for directing this dissertation, and to Hans Frei and George Lindbeck for their guidance and encouragement, though of course I bear sole responsibility for the conclusions contained herein. I am also indebted to David S.C. Kim, Chung Hwan Kwak, Edwin Ang, and Therese Stewart for their support. I wish to thank Kate Skrebutenas of the Speer Library, Princeton Theological Seminary, for her research assistance, the Division of Christian

Education of the National Council of Churches of Christ
in the U.S.A. for permission to quote from the Revised
Standard Version of the Bible, and the Princeton
University Library for permission to quote from the
Charles A. Hodge Collection. For valuable
conversations and suggestions, I am grateful to James
Fleming, Timothy Jackson, John Merrill, James Moorhead,
Robert Bruce Mullin, William Silva, Constantine
Tsirpanlis, Frank Turner, and John F. Wilson. Herbert
Mayr provided valuable assistance in preparing the
manuscript. My deepest gratitude, however, goes to my
wife, Lucy Wells, and my mother, Roberta Bidinger,
without whose tireless support and encouragement I
could not have finished.

PREFACE

According to a commonly received view, the central theological issue in the nineteenth-century Darwinian controversies was the argument from design. Princeton theologian Charles Hodge is often cited as a prominent example of this received view.

The basis of Hodge's opposition, however, was not the argument from design, but an argument to design: he believed in design because he believed in God, not in a God because he saw design. Consequently, Hodge saw Darwinism not merely as undercutting one possible source of knowledge about God, but as denying God's existence altogether.

This study evaluates the logic of Hodge's critique and examines his premises: by surveying the positions of some selected Christian theologians, it attempts to ascertain whether Hodge's argument to design was representative of Christianity as a whole; and by surveying the views of some nineteenth-century Darwinians, it attempts to evaluate Hodge's claim that Darwinism denies design. The survey finds that (1) the argument to design is a central element in mainstream Christian theology, and all the surveyed versions of it conclude that the human species was designed or intended by God; and (2) although Darwin thought his theory was compatible with a general notion of designed laws, he was convinced that it excluded design in any particular result, such as the human species.

The study concludes that: (1) Hodge's opposition to Darwinism based on the argument to design represents a major counter-example to the received view of the nineteenth-century Darwinian controversies; and (2) since the argument to design has evidently been much more central to mainstream Christian theology than the argument from design, the conceptual conflict between Christianity and Darwinism over the issue of design is broader and deeper than the received view implies.

CHAPTER ONE
Introduction: Religion Versus Science?

When John Draper published his *History of the Conflict Between Religion and Science* in 1873, he saw Christendom "in the midst of a controversy" over the doctrines of "Evolution, Creation, Development." Draper was convinced that science, "the expansive force of the human intellect," had always had to struggle against the "intellectual night" of religion. His polemic was directed primarily at the Roman Catholic Church and Vatican I, but he also singled out those Protestant denominations which had recently met in New York for the Sixth Conference of the Evangelical Alliance. Some participants at the Conference had publicly criticized the theory of evolution proposed by Charles Darwin, and Draper felt that the Alliance had thereby "averted its eyes from its ancient antagonist" (the Roman Catholic Church) and unwisely "fastened them, as the Vatican Council had done, on Science."[1]

Two decades later, Andrew White's *A History of the Warfare of Science with Theology in Christendom* refined Draper's approach in at least two respects: where Draper had regarded the conflict as one between science and religion, White narrowed it to "a struggle between Science and Dogmatic Theology;" and where Draper had made the Roman Catholic Church the main target of his polemic, White aimed his primary criticism at theological opposition to evolution. White traced belief in the Genesis creation narratives, Old Testament chronology, and the immutability of species from the early and medieval church to the nineteenth century, when the light of scientific progress promised to sweep away "outworn creeds and noxious dogmas." He thought he was witnessing "the last expiring convulsions of the old theologic theory" in the face of the new doctrine of evolution by natural selection.[2]

Though Draper's emphasis was institutional and White's theological, both were convinced that traditional Christianity had been opposing and obstructing science for centuries, and that the battle over evolution was merely the latest episode in a perennial war. The "warfare metaphor" of Draper and White, however, has been shown by recent historians to be seriously misleading in one respect, and overly simplistic in another. First, religion and science before Darwin, at least in Great Britain and the United States, were not so much in conflict as they were mutually supportive. A shared trust in Baconian empiricism lay at the basis of a "holy alliance of Newtonian science and Protestant religion" which remained largely intact until after Darwin published his *Origin of Species* in 1859.[3] Second, not even the Darwinian controversies were simply a war between science and religion, but involved a whole range of social, scientific, philosophical, and theological issues which pitted scientists against scientists and clergymen against clergymen, as well as scientists and clergymen against each other. Furthermore, a substantial number of clergymen and theologians readily embraced evolution, if not Darwin's particular theory.[4]

Nevertheless, a recognition of the misleading and simplistic nature of the warfare metaphor should not obscure the fact that 1859 initiated a period of very real conflict.

Of the social issues involved in the conflict, recent historians describe the "shift of authority and prestige" from the ecclesiastical to the scientific community in Great Britain, the "fading appeal of the Protestant churches for the working masses in the cities" in the United States, and the fear of disorientation and loss of identity which accompany the replacement of old beliefs with new.[5] These factors, and perhaps others like them, ought not to be ignored; but it would be a mistake, in the words of one reviewer, to "minimize the real intellectual struggle that was taking place."[6]

Of the intellectual issues involved in the controversy, some were scientific or philosophical rather than theological. Most scientists seem to have accepted the modern geological time scale by the time Darwin published the *Origin of Species*, but there were still disagreements over whether it included sufficient time to make Darwin's theory plausible. Furthermore, many people were philosophically committed to the immutability of species. Even among those scientists who by 1859 were convinced of the great age of the earth and were prepared to accept some form of evolution, many doubted whether Darwin's theory was supported by sufficient evidence, or whether natural selection was the true cause of the formation of species. Inseparable from these doubts were philosophical disputes over what constitutes sufficient evidence and true cause in science, and even over the nature of science itself.[7]

A major source of confusion, not only in the nineteenth-century controversies themselves but also in the secondary literature, was a widespread failure to distinguish between philosophical or biological evolution in general and Darwin's theory of natural selection in particular. In 1859, the principal proponent of philosophical evolution was Herbert Spencer, and the notion of biological evolution (usually referred to as "development") had already been advocated by Buffon, Lamarck, Chambers, and Erasmus Darwin, Charles Darwin's grandfather.[8] Perhaps in order to avoid confusion with these preexisting ideas, Darwin did not even use the word "evolution" in the *Origin of Species* (though the last word in the book is "evolved"), but preferred to use instead the somewhat more descriptive phrase "descent with modification."

Of the theological issues in the nineteenth-century Darwinian controversies, some historians maintain that the most significant was biblical: Darwin's theory challenged "belief in the historicity of Genesis."[9] Many others, however, would agree with a recent scholar who maintains that in the nineteenth century "there was little opposition to Darwinism on the grounds that it challenged the literal word of the Genesis creation story;"[10] and it may be that those who purport to see such opposition as a major factor are to some extent reading the biblical fundamentalism of twentieth-century creationist movements back into the earlier controversies.

Some historians regard "man's place in nature" as the central issue. Are human beings created in the

image of God, with immortal souls, or are they merely
the result of natural generation from lower animals?
Evolution seemed to cause "the demotion of man from his
august position in the universe."[11] Other scholars,
however, claim that although this issue was prominent
at the popular level it was not the main focus of
debate among intellectuals. One study of the British
controversies concludes that "to the uneducated
majority the question was simply whether man was
descended from Adam or from the apes," but that "on a
higher educational level" the issue was whether God
intervenes miraculously in natural processes or leaves
them to operate autonomously. According to another
writer, the principal criticism of Darwin's theory at
the New York Evangelical Alliance Conference in 1873
was that its naturalism was "utterly incompatible" with
"the supernaturalism of the Biblical view."[12]

Other recent studies of the Darwinian
controversies, perhaps even a majority of them,
maintain that the central theological issue was design.
The same survey of the British controversies which
finds human origins to be the focus at one level, and
miraculous intervention the focus at another, concludes
that a more fundamental conflict involved the
"teleological interpretation of nature which lies at
the root of practically any sort of religious belief."
As one writer puts it, "the role of divine Providence
in the course of nature was the central issue," because
"Darwin's theory was necessarily fatal to the idea of
God as craftsman and governor."[13]

Of those historians who consider design to have
been the central issue, most maintain that the
controversy was due to a conflict between Darwinism and

the teleological argument for the existence of God, also known as the argument from design. Evidence of design or order in the world is taken to imply the existence of a designer, and this designer, it is argued, must be God. The argument from design has been attributed by various writers to Plato, Aristotle, and the Stoics, though it appears to have first been used as a theistic proof by the Jewish philosopher Philo in the first century before Christ.[14] Christian theologians, however, made little use of the argument for the first seventeen centuries, with the notable exception of two relatively brief references to it by Thomas Aquinas. Aquinas argued in his *Summa Theologiae* that "natural bodies act for an end," in the sense that they act "always, or nearly always, in the same way, so as to obtain the best result," and therefore "some intelligent being exists by whom all natural things are directed to their end." In his *Summa Contra Gentiles*, Aquinas argued that since "things of diverse natures come together under one order" in the world, there must exist "some being by whose providence the world is governed."[15] Except for these brief references by Aquinas, the design argument of the ancient Greeks (according to one standard history) was "virtually ignored by Medieval thought," and "in effect leaped a thousand years" to reemerge "in the theological lists of the Enlightenment."[16]

In the late seventeenth century, however, the argument from design began rising to prominence among English-speaking theologians. For a century and a half, British and American scientists (many of whom were also clergymen) studied natural phenomena with two purposes in mind: to gain useful knowledge, and to find evidence for Christian beliefs. Natural theology flourished, basing its doctrinal claims largely on the argument from design, and in the process encouraging extensive scientific research, though mainly of a descriptive character. This tendency reached its peak in Britain with the publication of William Paley's *Natural Theology* in 1802, and the publication of the eight *Bridgewater Treatises* three decades later. Paley argued that just as someone who finds a watch infers that it was constructed by a watchmaker, so anyone who observes the evidence of design in nature must acknowledge a wise and benevolent creator. The anatomy and physiology of an animal, especially, are so perfectly adapted to the needs of the organism that they afford ample evidence of design, and Paley and the authors of several of the *Bridgewater Treatises* point to hundreds of examples of such adaptations.[17]

The Darwinian controversies in Britain and America took place in this context. Darwin's theory seemed to undercut natural theology by offering an explanation for the origin of adaptations which was independent of, and perhaps even incompatible with, divine design. Many (perhaps most) recent historians identify this as the single most important theological issue in the nineteenth-century controversies. According to this commonly received view, religious opposition arose primarily because of a perception that Darwinism "questioned", "threatened", "contradicted", or even "demolished" the argument from design.[18]

The argument from design, however, had already been questioned, threatened, contradicted, and (some would even say) demolished by the philosophical critiques of Hume and Kant several years before Paley

published his *Natural Theology*. Hume and Kant had
criticized the argument on two grounds: first, living
organisms are not analogous to human contrivances,
since the former seem to order themselves from within
rather than to have order imposed on them from without;
and second, even if the analogy between nature and
contrivance were valid, the argument would prove only
the existence of a designer, not the omnipotent and
loving God of Christianity. Paley disagreed on both
counts, but instead of attempting to meet the
philosophical challenge posed by Hume and Kant he
largely ignored it, devoting himself to cataloguing and
describing what he considered to be evidences of design
in nature. The same could be said for Anglo-American
natural theology in general, and it was not until
Darwin provided an alternative explanation for the
organic adaptations which made up the bulk of Paley's
examples that natural theology lost its wide appeal.[19]

If the received view is correct, and the
fundamental theological objection to Darwinism in the
nineteenth-century controversies was its perceived
incompatibility with the argument from design, then for
Christianity as a whole those controversies would
appear to be of rather limited interest. Since the
popularity of the argument from design was largely
restricted to Britain and America in the eighteenth and
nineteenth centuries, since many modern theologians
consider the philosophical critiques of Hume and Kant a
more fundamental challenge than Darwin's theory, and
since even twentieth-century creationism relies
primarily on a fundamentalist interpretation of Genesis
rather than on the argument from design, it seems that
the major theological issue in the nineteenth-century

Darwinian controversies has little relevance for
Christian theology as a whole.

Some scholars, however, would be unwilling to
dismiss the issue so readily. First, there are hints
that proving the existence and attributes of God was
not the only way design functioned theologically in the
Darwinian controversies. According to one writer, "in
the form some theologians gave the argument, God was
taken for granted, and design inferred from his
existence." In other words, some people argued from
God's existence to design, rather than to God's
existence from design. The distinction between the two
ways of reasoning was succinctly stated by John Henry
Newman: "I believe in design because I believe in God;
not in a God because I see design."[20]

Second, some historians are convinced that the
issues in the nineteenth-century controversies have
never been sufficiently clarified. One recent study
concludes that "in a basic sense the issue with Darwin
was hardly joined," and the debate remains "confused
and unfinished." Another recent writer suggests that
"the course of interactions between theology and modern
science remains uncharted," and that many issues of
theological concern "remain largely unidentified."
Still another recommends "new investigations," and
"full-blooded contextual analyses" of the doctrines
involved in the controversies. Clearly, there is a
need for more work in clarifying the nature of the
theological conflicts.[21]

An attempt at clarification could take either one
of two general approaches: it could carefully
distinguish the different positions of various
partisans in the controversies, or it could examine in

depth the theological position of a particular
individual. Since most good historical work in recent
years has taken the former approach, there seems to be
more of a need for the latter; and if one particular
individual is to be studied, it seems reasonable to
choose a prominent theologian who opposed Darwin's
theory. In nineteenth-century America, the obvious
choice would be Charles Hodge, of Princeton Theological
Seminary. Although Draper's *History of the Conflict
Between Religion and Science* did not mention him by
name, Hodge was the most implacable foe of Darwinism at
the 1873 New York Evangelical Alliance Conference that
Draper singled out for criticism; and White's *History
of the Warfare of Science with Theology in Christendom*
placed Hodge at the top of the list of religious
opponents of evolution in the United States. One
twentieth-century historian even maintains, with only a
little exaggeration, that the Darwinian controversies
in America were merely skirmishes until "the grand
battle was joined" with the publication of Hodge's *What
Is Darwinism?* in 1874.[22]

Although Hodge's prominence as an opponent of
Darwinism is generally conceded, twentieth-century
estimates of the nature and quality of his opposition
vary widely. On the one hand, Hodge is described as
"not a man to entertain new ideas," and it may even be
"doubted if he was capable of understanding them." One
historian, surveying religious opposition to Darwinism
in Hodge's *Biblical Repertory and Princeton Review* and
other periodicals, finds it "difficult not to be weary
or impatient" with the "dismal exhibition of arrogance"
by "fundamentalist writers." Though not mentioning
Hodge by name, this same historian concludes from his

survey that "these volumes" contain "rationalizations unworthy of a sophomoric intelligence" and "arguments conceived in utter defiance of logic." Other writers call Hodge a biblical fundamentalist who defended "the Sunday School God", or they attribute his anti-Darwinian stand to advanced age and a belligerent attitude.[23]

On the other hand, one recent scholar considers estimates like these to be "marred by the tendency to make pro-Darwin forces the good guys and anti-Darwinians the incarnation of evil." Apparently managing to avoid this tendency, one historian describes Hodge as "probably the foremost theologian of his day," whose opposition to Darwinism was "on a much higher plane" than most popular reactions. One study portrays him as "anything but a simple minded man," with "an intellect surpassed by few in his day." According to another writer surveying religious opposition to Darwinism, Hodge's *What Is Darwinism?* was "probably the best statement of this view by an Anglo-Saxon Protestant." Still another calls the book "perceptive and even-tempered," and considers Hodge to be "among Darwin's more discerning critics on both sides of the Atlantic."[24]

Given the confusion over the nature of the theological conflicts, and the contradictory evaluations of Hodge's contribution to them, a careful study of Hodge's theological opposition to Darwinism is definitely in order. Indeed, one recent reviewer concludes that since most writers "slight those Americans -- undoubtedly the majority -- who resisted Darwin's theories," a "systematic and sympathetic study of such persons is long overdue."[25] The objective of the present study, however, is primarily to clarify theological issues in the Darwinian controversies, and only secondarily to provide a sympathetic reevaluation of Hodge. The emphasis here is thus theological rather than historical; but since this particular theological issue is probably best studied in its historical context, the analysis of it is preceded by a review of the intellectual background of Hodge's critique.

NOTES

1.   Draper, *History of the Conflict Between Religion and Science*, vi-vii, x, xv, 352-354.

2.   Andrew White, *History of the Warfare of Science with Theology in Christendom*, v-ix, 1-88;   Edward White, *Science and Religion in American Thought*, 9-11, 30-35.

3.   Bozeman, *Protestants in an Age of Science*, 164-167.   See also Borome, "Evolution Controversy," 169-170;   Daniels, *American Science in the Age of Jackson*, 190-200;   Gillispie, *Genesis and Geology*, 184-216;   Hooykaas, *Religion and the Rise of Modern Science*, 98-149;   Hovenkamp, *Science and Religion in America*, xi;   Klaaren, *Religious Origins of Modern Science*, 27, 185-191.

4.   Daniels, *Darwinism Comes to America*, xvi-xvii, 95;   Hofstadter, *Development of Academic Freedom in the United States*, 344-350;   Livingston, "Darwin, Darwinism, and Theology," 114-115;   Moore, *Post-Darwinian Controversies*, 1216, 346351;   Numbers, "Science and Religion," 75;   Ruse, *Darwinian Revolution*, 239-241, 271-272;   Welch, *Protestant Thought in the Nineteenth Century*, 2:183-184;   David Wilson, "Darwin and the Protestants," 200.

5.   Turner, "Victorian Conflict between Science and Religion," 356-359;   Hofstadter, *Development of Academic Freedom in the United States*, 322-325.   See also Borome, "Evolution Controversy," 179-181;   Peckham, *Triumph of Romanticism*, 193.

6.   Livingston, "Darwin, Darwinism, and Theology," 114.

7.   Bowler, *Evolution: History of an Idea*, 176-205;   Ellegard, "Darwinian Theory and Nineteenth-century Philosophies of Science," 362-393;   Moore, *Post-Darwinian Controversies*, 214-215;   Ruse, *Darwinian Revolution*, 36-63, 234-239.

8. Aldrich, "United States: Bibliographical Essay,"
207; Barzun, *Darwin, Marx, Wagner*, 38-47; Borome,
"Evolution Controversy," 172; Bowler, Evolution:
History of an Idea, 46-84; Livingston, "Darwin,
Darwinism, and Theology," 112; Parkinson, "Charles
Darwin's Influence on Religion," 13-19; Peckham,
Triumph of Romanticism, 178-188.

9. Greene, *Darwin and the Modern World View*, 37. See
also Marsden, "Creation versus Evolution," 571-572;
Lack, *Evolutionary Theory and Christian Belief*, 16.

10. Bowler, *Evolution: History of an Idea*, 206. See
also Pfeifer, "United States," 182; Welch, *Protestant
Thought in the Nineteenth Century*, 2:187-192.

11. Young, *Darwin's Metaphor*, 9; Borome, "Evolution
Controversy," 171.

12. Ellegard, *Darwin and the General Reader*, 332-335;
Marsden, *Fundamentalism and American Culture*, 19.

13. Ellegard, *Darwin and the General Reader*, 332-335;
Gillispie, *Genesis and Geology*, 220. See also
Hovenkamp, *Science and Religion in America*, xi, 190;
Welch, *Protestant Thought in the Nineteenth Century*,
2:192-193;

14. Dupre, *Dubious Heritage*, 152-153; Hurlbutt, *Hume,
Newton, and the Design Argument*, 95-126; McPherson,
Argument from Design, 1.

15. Aquinas, *Summa Theologica* Ia, q. 2, art. 3;
Aquinas, *Summa Contra Gentiles* bk. 1, chap. 13.

16. Hurlbutt, Hume, *Newton, and the Design Argument*,
126.

17. Cupitt, "Darwinism and English Religious Thought,"
125-126; Eiseley, *Darwin's Century*, 14-16, 174-178;
Gillispie, *Genesis and Geology*, 19-20, 35-40, 104-106,
195-196, 209-219; Greene, *Death of Adam*, 110.

18. Gary Smith, "Calvinists and Evolution," 337;
Bowler, *Evolution: History of an Idea*, 210; Russett,
Darwin in America, 12; Gillespie, *Charles Darwin and
the Problem of Creation*, 83. See also Cupitt,
"Darwinism and English Religious Thought," 125-127;
Daniels, *Darwinism Comes to America*, xv; Davis,
"Presbyterian Attitudes Toward Science," 25, 28, 33;

Dupree, *Asa Gray*, 375; Ellegard, "Darwinian Theory and the Argument from Design," 173-187; Greene, *Darwin and the Modern World View*, 39-45; Lack, *Evolutionary Theory and Christian Belief*, 16; Livingstone, "Idea of Design," 330-337, 342; Loewenberg, "Controversy over Evolution," 247; Loewenberg, "Impact of the Doctrine of Evolution," 85; McGiffert, "Christian Darwinism," 176, 195; Marsden, *Fundamentalism and American Culture*, 16-17; Persons, *Evolutionary Thought in America*, 426; Pfeifer, "United States," 182.

19. Ellegard, *Darwin and the General Reader*, 114-117; Hume, *Dialogues Concerning Natural Religion*, pts. 57; Kant, *Critique of Pure Reason*, 518-524; Paley, *Natural Theology*, 309-310, 329-330; N. K. Smith, *Commentary to Kant's 'Critique of Pure Reason'*, 538-540.

20. Ellegard, *Darwin and the General Reader*, 125; Newman, *Letters and Diaries*, 25:97. See also Dillenberger, *Protestant Thought and Natural Science*, 241.

21. Welch, *Protestant Thought in the Nineteenth Century*, 2:210-211; Numbers, "Science and Religion," 79; Moore, "Creation and the Problem of Charles Darwin," 196. See also Lack, *Evolutionary Theory and Christian Belief*, 9.

22. Livingston, "Darwin, Darwinism, and Theology," 112; Draper, *History of the Conflict Between Religion and Science*, 352-353; Andrew White, *History of the Warfare of Science with Theology*, 86; Foster, *Modern Movement in American Theology*, 43; Numbers, "Science and Religion," 73.

23. Foster, *Modern Movement in American Theology*, 4748; Loewenberg, "Controversy Over Evolution," 234, 247, 257; Goodman & Goodman, "Creation and Evolution," 14-16. See also Borome, "Evolution Controversy," 184-186; Johnson, "Attitudes of the Princeton Theologians Toward Darwinism," 106, 289; Hovenkamp, *Science and Religion in America*, 212; Pfeifer, "Reception of Darwinism," 71-72, 144.

24. Aldrich, "United States: Bibliographical Essay," 208; Russett, *Darwin in America*, 26; Berg, "Charles A. Hodge, Controversialist," 38; Welch, *Protestant Thought in the Nineteenth Century*, 2:198; Moore, *Post-Darwinian Controversies*, 203, 214. See also Dillenberger, *Protestant Thought and Natural Science*,

234; Gillespie, *Charles Darwin and the Problem of Creation*, 112; Marsden, *Fundamentalism and American Culture*, 119; Numbers, "Science and Religion," 77-78.

25. Numbers, "Science and Religion," 76. See also Borome, "Evolution Controversy," 190-191.

CHAPTER TWO
The Background: Hodge Before Darwin

Charles Hodge was born in Philadelphia in 1797, to devoutly Presbyterian parents. His father died when he was only a year old, and he was raised thereafter by his mother, who took the family to church regularly and drilled them at home in the Westminster Catechism. Hodge later recalled that as a boy he prayed frequently, "walking along the streets, in school and out of school, whether playing or studying." It "seemed natural" to do so, since he "thought of God as an everywhere-present Being, full of kindness and love, who would not be offended if children talked to him." In retrospect, he considered this a "mild form of natural religion," not unlike "the worship rendered by the fowls of the air."[1]

In 1812, Hodge went to Princeton to study at the College of New Jersey. The College had been founded by Presbyterians; and ever since 1768, when its trustees had brought Presbyterian minister John Witherspoon from Scotland to be its president, the Scottish philosophy of common sense had been an important element in the intellectual life of the school. Princeton was far from unique in this respect, since by Hodge's time the Scottish philosophy had also been introduced at Harvard, Yale, and Andover, and was becoming widely influential in American thought. The combination of

Presbyterian theology with Scottish philosophy (which relied heavily on the inductive method of Francis Bacon) helped to promote the growth of natural science in early nineteenth-century America; and the sciences were prominent in the Princeton curriculum during this period.[2]

When revivalism swept the Princeton campus in 1815, Hodge underwent something of a conversion experience; and upon his graduation the following year he entered Princeton Seminary, which, like the College, had been founded by Presbyterians. Hodge's principal mentor at the Seminary was Professor Archibald Alexander, a Presbyterian minister. According to Hodge's son and biographer, Alexander "expressed great favor" for the Scottish philosophy and "rendered due homage" to Paley's *Natural Theology*. The primary textbook for Alexander's students, however, was the *Institutio Theologiae Elencticae* of Francis Turretin, a seventeenth-century Calvinist scholastic. Although Alexander often dissented from Turretin on specific points, the *Institutio* furnished the basic framework for Hodge's theological education.[3]

After graduating from Princeton Seminary in 1819, Hodge was ordained by the Presbyterian Church, and widened his education by attending lectures on anatomy and physiology. In 1822, he married Sarah Bache and became Professor of Biblical and Oriental Literature at the Seminary. Three years later, Hodge founded the *Biblical Repertory*, a journal designed to "assist ministers and laymen in the criticism and interpretation of the Bible." The following year he obtained permission from the Seminary to study in Europe, where he was exposed first-hand to German

philosophy, natural science, biblical criticism, and
theology. He disliked German theology in general, and
Schleiermacher's theology in particular, because he
felt that it was dominated by speculative philosophy
rather than biblical religion.[4]

In 1828, Hodge returned to Princeton. The
following year, he reorganized his journal as the
Biblical Repertory and Theological Review (later
renamed the *Biblical Repertory and Princeton Review*),
dedicating it to "a right understanding" of the Bible.
Its task was "to bring under strict, impartial review
the philosophy and literature of the time," exposing
"the error of founding religious doctrines on isolated
passages" or of "forcing the Scriptures to a meaning
which shall accord with philosophical theories." Years
later, after having served as the journal's primary
editor and most prolific contributor for four decades,
Hodge would characterize this task as "the vindication
of that system of doctrine" which is "contained in the
Westminster Confession of Faith."[5]

When Hodge was appointed Professor of Didactic
Theology at the Seminary in 1840, he continued to use
Turretin's *Institutio* as his textbook. Before one
class meeting each week, he would assign a topic and
corresponding section of the *Institutio* in Latin. The
class meeting would then consist of a thorough
discussion of this subject in the form of question and
answer, during which Hodge strove to force each student
to do his own thinking. The second class meeting that
week would consist of a lecture by Hodge on the same
topic. The following week, students would be required
to submit written answers to a list of questions on
that topic, drawing their answers from Turretin,

Hodge's lectures, or other materials in the Seminary
library. In this process, the *Institutio* was not
taught by rote, nor did Hodge's views always coincide
with Turretin's; but it is clear that seventeenth-
century Calvinist scholasticism played a prominent role
in Hodge's teaching.[6]

It would be a mistake, however, to think of Hodge
as a merely academic theologian. He continued to
preach, and the notes of many of his sermons have been
preserved. He also took an active part in the pastoral
conferences between professors and students which were
held at Princeton Seminary every Sunday afternoon. At
those conferences, academic theology "gave place to the
warmth of personal religious experience;" and among
those present (according to one of his students), "Dr.
Hodge's was the voice which all waited to hear."
Hodge's personal piety and fatherly concern inspired
deep love and admiration in many of the more than three
thousand students he taught in the course of his long
career.[7] According to one recent writer, Hodge was "an
almost classic realization of the kneeling, as opposed
to sitting, theologian."[8]

Nevertheless, for the purpose of this essay it is
Hodge's academic theology which is of primary interest.
As that theology developed, it was obviously influenced
by the Calvinism of the Westminster Confession and
Turretin's *Institutio*. Less obviously, but no less
surely, it was influenced by Scottish common-sense
philosophy, which in turn relied heavily on the
inductivism of Francis Bacon. It was also influenced
by the sort of natural theology exemplified by Paley's
work.[9] Before turning to a consideration of Hodge's
theology, then, it seems worthwhile to review these

influences briefly. Since all of them have been
treated in detail by other writers, what follows is not
intended to be a thorough discussion, but merely a
summary of some selected aspects which are particularly
relevant to Hodge's critique of Darwinism.

(1) Theological Influences

Like the other reformers of the sixteenth century,
John Calvin reacted against Roman ecclesiasticism by
appealing to the authority of scripture. Believers
should read the Bible "as if" they were hearing the
very words of God. In his *Institutes of the Christian
Religion* and his biblical commentaries, Calvin
sometimes writes as though scripture had been dictated
from heaven; and he believes, in a general way, in the
factual and historical veracity of the Old and New
Testaments. On the other hand, Calvin is not
especially interested in chronology, nor in historical
or geographical details; and he concedes that the
biblical writers sometimes accommodated themselves to
popular misconceptions. In other words, although
Calvin considers the whole of the Bible to be divinely
inspired, it seems that he does not hold a mechanical
theory of inspiration whereby every word is dictated
and thus inerrant. Scripture is an imperfect "mirror"
of the truth rather than the truth itself; but this is
sufficient for faith, because faith is not so much an
intellectual assent to facts and propositions as it is
a trusting obedience to God's redemptive will, produced
by the inward working of the Holy Spirit.[10]

What scripture teaches, nevertheless, is "knowledge
of God," though such knowledge involves all the
spiritual faculties and not just the intellect.

According to Calvin, if the fall had not occurred, knowledge of God could have been learned from the structure of the world and from the human mind; but because of the corruption caused by the fall, such knowledge cannot now be attained without the aid of the Bible. Not only is scripture necessary for knowledge of God the Redeemer, but also for knowledge of God the Creator. Although God's wisdom and power are still sufficiently perceptible in nature and history to render people "inexcusable," the blindness of sin requires that people use the "spectacles" of scripture to see God's natural revelation clearly. This does not mean that one relies only on the Bible to learn about nature and history, but that the Bible enables one to understand them correctly. Once we are equipped with the spectacles of scripture, "the universe is for us a sort of mirror in which we can contemplate God, who is otherwise invisible." Although God's glory then becomes evident even to "the most untutored," it is advantageous to "investigate the motion of the stars" and "the structure of the human body," since "God's providence shows itself more explicitly when one observes these." Calvin's theology thus encourages scientific investigation, so long as it is pursued with the proper faith.[11]

The content of this faith consists, above all, in an awareness of God's transcendent sovereignty. All things visible and invisible are totally dependent on God's will, not only for their initial creation but also for their continuing governance. Calvin does not deny the existence of secondary natural causes, except in the initial act of creation; nor does he deny the basic orderliness of the universe. He insists,

however, that God is not bound by those causes or that
orderliness, but instead actively controls them.
Chance and fate are ruled out. At every instant,
natural processes are subservient to the will of God.[12]

A century after Calvin had published his *Institutes
of the Christian Religion*, an assembly of English
Calvinists was commissioned by Parliament to formulate
a confession of faith. The resulting Westminster
Confession represents a theological consensus of the
Reformed Churches in the mid-seventeenth century, a
summary of classical Calvinism as it had been refined
by a century of doctrinal controversies. The
Confession begins by affirming that although the "light
of nature" sufficiently manifests God's "goodness,
wisdom, and power" to render people "inexcusable," only
scripture provides the knowledge of God which is
necessary for salvation. Scripture can be trusted
because God was its author, having "immediately
inspired" both the Old and New Testaments; and
believers are persuaded of its "infallible truth" by
"the inward work of the Holy Spirit." Among the truths
taught by scripture are the creation by God of all
things visible and invisible "in the space of six
days," and God's providential government of "all
creatures, actions, and things." Ordinarily, God's
providence makes use of means, but God is "free to work
without, above, and against them, at his pleasure."
Although the Westminster Confession lost its authority
in England when the monarchy was restored in 1660, it
became the doctrinal standard for Scottish and American
Presbyterians.[13] The Confession was accompanied by a
Shorter Catechism consisting of questions and answers

for the religious instruction of children; and it was this Catechism which Hodge memorized as a boy.[14]

Compared with earlier Reformed confessions, the Westminster Confession tends to be somewhat more rational and precise. According to Philip Schaff (a contemporary of Hodge), the Confession goes too far in this respect, being more of a "scientific treatise of theology" than a "public confession of faith." To whatever extent this is true, it seems to have been due largely to the influence of seventeenth-century Calvinist scholastics, one of whom was Francis Turretin of Geneva.[15]

Turretin's *Institutio Theologiae Elencticae* is patterned roughly after the *Summa Theologiae* of Thomas Aquinas. Topics are divided into questions, each of which is followed by articles elaborating the correct (i.e., Calvinist) answer and refuting various objections. Under the first topic, which deals with the nature of theology, Turretin maintains that people possess an innate knowledge of God which is sufficient to convince them that God exists and ought to be worshipped, but which is insufficient for salvation. Reason, not as corrupted by sin but as "healed by grace," is useful in theology as an instrument of argumentation, explanation, and the defense of orthodoxy, and even as an aid to draw people to faith; but reason is not the principle or rule of faith, and must therefore not be expected to comprehend fully the "mysteries of faith," much less be presumed competent to pass judgement on them. The "first and infallible standard" of faith, and the source of saving knowledge, is not reason but scripture, as interpreted under the guidance of the Holy Spirit.[16]

According to Turretin, the biblical writers were "so acted upon and inspired by the Holy Spirit, both as to the things themselves and as to the words, as to be kept free from all error." The books of the Bible, which "have God for their author," are thus "the divine and infallible truth," even in historical details.[17] To some extent, these claims had also been made by Calvin; but in Calvin's theology they were balanced by a greater awareness of the historically conditioned character of the text. As Schaff puts it, Calvinist scholastics such as Turretin "departed from the more liberal view of the Reformers on the mode and degree of inspiration," substituting for it "a rigid mechanical theory which ignored the human and historical aspect" and reduced the biblical writers to "mere penmen" of the Holy Spirit. This led to a tendency to absolutize the text which culminated in the Helvetic Consensus Formula of 1675. The Formula, which Turretin helped to compose, affirmed the divine inspiration of the Hebrew vowel-points in the Old Testament and thereby excluded textual criticism, which had already demonstrated a relatively recent origin for the Hebrew system of vocalization. The biblical text, thus absolutized, became in Turretin's hands a source of detailed historical information as well as of the knowledge of God. For example, although he acknowledges that it is not doctrinally necessary to decide the matter, he deduces that the six days of creation probably took place in the autumn.[18]

The sixth topic in the *Institutio* deals with God's providence. Like Calvin, Turretin defends providence against both fate and chance. Providence, which "cannot be wholly denied, without at the same time denying God," wisely and powerfully directs "all things, even the smallest." In order to reconcile God's providence with the integrity of secondary natural causes, Turretin adopts Aquinas' theory of concursus, which considers God the immediate cause of all actions of created beings, directing them toward their final end without destroying contingency or free will. This last point is elaborated by means of complex scholastic argumentation. It is this rationalistic style of doing theology, together with his overly mechanical approach to scripture, rather than any specific doctrinal differences, which most sharply distinguish Turretin from Calvin.[19]

During the century and a half following Turretin, another sort of rationalistic tendency rose to prominence in English theology: the tendency to deduce God's existence and attributes from evidence of design in nature, without resorting to scripture at all. The most widely influential example of this tendency was William Paley's *Natural Theology* (1802), which makes extensive use of detailed examples from the natural sciences to justify the claim that nature exhibits design. Theologically, the principal significance of Paley's approach is that it tends to treat natural knowledge of God as directly accessible through scientific observation, without the aid of scripture. To be sure, Paley felt that the "more personal" mode of communication used in scripture "suits the span of our intellects much better" than deriving the knowledge of God from nature; but the Calvinist insistence that sin renders scripture necessary for knowledge of God is not to be found in Paley's *Natural Theology*.[20]

Paley's influence, however, was a relatively minor factor in Hodge's theological inheritance. The major factor was the Reformers' faith in scripture as the source of true knowledge of God and as the starting-point for theology. What Hodge inherited was a faith in scripture which was less spiritualistic and more rationalistic than Calvin's; but it was still a faith in scripture rather than a faith in the self-sufficiency of human reason. A second major factor in Hodge's theological inheritance was the Calvinist faith that nature and history are governed by God's providence. Whatever human investigation may discover about natural processes must be interpreted in light of the fundamental truth that such processes are guided by God for a divine purpose. A third major factor was a profound confidence in the harmony of natural science and religion. Since God was both the creator of the world and the author of the Bible, it was inconceivable that there could be any contradiction between nature and scripture.

(2) Philosophical Influences

The major philosophical influences on Hodge's theology, or at least those most written about in recent years, were Baconianism and Scottish common-sense realism. In a sense, the two were not really distinct for Hodge, since the latter relied on the inductivism of the former, and since the former reached nineteenth-century America largely through the mediation of the latter; but historically, the two were a century apart.

In the early seventeenth century, Francis Bacon reacted against the abstract Aristotelianism which his

generation had inherited from medieval philosophy.
Bacon claims that knowledge is worth pursuing primarily
because of its usefulness, its true purpose being to
extend human dominion over nature. He divides natural
philosophy into two categories, "practical" (roughly
equivalent to "applied science" today), and
"speculative." In the latter category, Bacon assigns
the study of what he calls material and efficient
causes to "physics" (roughly equivalent to
"experimental and theoretical science" today), and the
study of what he calls formal and final causes to
"metaphysics." Although Bacon does not deny the
existence of final causes, much less "the fountain of
final causes, namely God," he is convinced that they
have no useful place in the study of nature. According
to Bacon, "the inquisition of Final Causes is barren,
and like a virgin consecrated to God produces nothing."
Their application to the study of nature hinders "the
diligent inquiry of physical causes," to the "great
arrest and prejudice of science." Nevertheless, if
final and physical causes "be but kept within their
proper bounds," Bacon is confident that there is no
"enmity or repugnancy at all between the two."[21]

Since Bacon feels that the value of knowledge
depends on its capacity to produce practical effects,
and since practical effects are produced only by real
physical causes, Bacon elaborates a method for gaining
knowledge of physical causes. His method is
"induction," whereby an interpreter of nature begins by
carefully observing particular cases, then proceeds "to
educe and form axioms from experience" and then "to
deduce and derive new experiments from axioms." In
modern terminology, Baconian inductivism formulates

hypotheses based on observations, then devises
experiments to test consequences deduced from the
hypotheses. It is not enough merely to collect
observations or multiply experiments: Bacon sees
induction as an active intellectual effort which goes
beyond the data to discover their "forms" (roughly
equivalent, in modern terminology, to natural laws
which govern physical behavior). On the other hand,
Bacon seems to conceive of his method as a rather
mechanical tool which could be successfully employed by
anyone of ordinary intelligence. In comparison with
many twentieth-century philosophers of science, Bacon
thus largely ignores the role of imaginative genius in
formulating scientific theories.[22]

A century after Bacon had developed his inductive
method as a reaction against medieval Aristotelianism,
Scottish Presbyterian Thomas Reid appealed to
inductivism as the basis of his philosophy of common
sense, which he developed in reaction to the skepticism
of David Hume. Reid maintains that Hume's skepticism
was a logical consequence of the theory, common among
philosophers, that knowledge of extramental phenomena
is mediated through mental representations called
ideas. According to Reid, it is a mistake to reason by
analogy from matter to mind, and thereby to reify
mental operations as ideas. These shadowy
intermediaries between thinking and the objects of
thought not only lead to philosophical paradoxes but
are also unnecessary, since the problem they were
intended to solve can be solved more simply by assuming
the immediacy of perception, memory, and thought.
Besides, when Reid adapted Bacon's inductive method to

the introspective study of his own mind, he found no evidence of such intermediaries.[23]

What Reid did profess to find, however, were some principles "which the constitution of our nature leads us to believe, and which we are under a necessity to take for granted in the common concerns of life, without being able to give a reason for them." These principles, which are prior to and independent of experience (and with which, presumably, we were endowed by God), Reid calls "the principles of common sense." They include the real existence of objects perceived by the senses, the real existence of the self and other selves, the efficacy of human agency, the certainty that intelligence in the cause can be inferred from design in the effect, and so on. Such principles are universal, in the sense that they are taken for granted in human conduct in general, and are reflected in the structure of all languages. Common-sense principles are also necessary, in the sense that to think the contrary is not only false but also absurd; and even those philosophers who do manage to think the contrary continue to act (if they are sane) as though they were true. There may be disagreement about this or that particular principle, but reason goes astray when it doubts common sense per se.[24]

Reid's philosophy suffers from a confusion between practical necessity and philosophical necessity (i.e., the suggestion that because a principle is taken for granted in human conduct its contrary must be logically absurd). Furthermore, it is questionable whether Reid understood Hume's position correctly. Nevertheless, it seems unfair to charge him (as Kant did) with a vulgar "appeal to the opinion of the multitude." Reid, like

Kant after him, was attempting to refute skepticism by discovering the fundamental principles by which the human mind operates. Apart from the much greater sophistication of Kant's critiques, probably the most notable difference between the two is that Reid believes it is possible to have direct knowledge of extramental reality.[25]

Reid's philosophy, especially as expounded by Dugald Stewart, found a ready audience in the United States. By appealing to Baconian inductivism to refute Humean skepticism, Scottish common-sense realism seemed ideally suited both to defend religion and to confirm its harmony with science, which likewise relied on the inductive method. It is not surprising, therefore, that Reid's philosophy became a dominant influence in nineteenth century American thought.[26] What Hodge inherited from this philosophical tradition was above all a profound confidence in the inductive method. It seemed to yield reliable knowledge in each of two very distinct realms, nature and mind. When applied to the former, it provided useful scientific knowledge of physical causes; when applied to the latter, it disclosed universal and necessary principles of thought which could provide a basis for certain religious claims. A tension remained, however, with respect to the notion of design: the inductive study of mind revealed the common-sense principle that intelligence in the cause could be inferred from design in the effect, but the Baconian method had no use for the notion of design in the study of nature.

(3) Hodge's Theology

Shaped by the theological and philosophical influences described above, Hodge's theology found its fullest and most mature expression in his *Systematic Theology,* published in three volumes from 1871 to 1873. Since the first volume contains the theological foundation for Hodge's critique of Darwinism, with which the second volume begins, what follows is primarily a review of the relevant sections in Volume I of *Systematic Theology*. This includes those sections dealing with the role of scripture and reason in theology, the teleological argument for God's existence, and the doctrines of creation and providence.

Hodge begins his *Systematic Theology* with a distinction which figures prominently in his thinking: "In every science there are two factors: facts and ideas." Both are essential, since the mere orderly arrangement of facts does not amount to science, which must go beyond isolated facts to exhibit their internal relations and to "understand the laws by which the facts of experience are determined." The truths of the Bible are the facts of theological science, though the Bible "is no more a system of theology, than nature is a system of chemistry or mechanics." Nevertheless, God "gives us in the Bible the truths which, properly understood and arranged, constitute the science of theology." Theology, then, is "the exhibition of the facts of Scripture in their proper order and relation, with the principles or general truths involved in the facts themselves, and which pervade and harmonize the whole."[27]

According to Hodge, the various methods used in theology "may, perhaps, be reduced to three general classes:" speculative, mystical, and inductive. The speculative method "assumes, in an _a priori_ manner, certain principles, and from them undertakes to determine what is and what must be." This rationalistic or dogmatic approach tends to make the human mind the measure of truth, and inevitably distorts the teachings of the Bible. The mystical method relies on feelings or intuitions rather than reason; but like the speculative method, it tends to neglect the scriptures. Hodge considers the best method to be inductive, which is "so called because it agrees in everything essential with the inductive method as applied to the natural sciences." Just as the natural scientist "comes to the study of nature with certain assumptions" about the trustworthiness of sense perceptions and mental operations, so the theologian "must assume the validity of those laws of belief which God has impressed upon our nature;" just as the scientist proceeds from these assumptions to "perceive, gather, and combine his facts," so it is the duty of the theologian "to ascertain, collect, and combine all the facts which God has revealed concerning himself and our relation to Him;" and just as the scientist deduces from the facts "the laws by which they are determined," so for the theologian "principles are derived from facts, and not impressed upon them." The truths of the Bible, like the facts of nature, "bear a natural relation to each other, which cannot be overlooked or perverted without the facts themselves being perverted." Therefore, the theologian "can no more construct a system of theology to suit his fancy,

than the astronomer can adjust the mechanism of the
heavens according to his own good pleasure." For
example, it is "unscientific for the theologian to
assume a theory as to the nature of virtue, of sin, of
liberty, of moral obligation, and then explain the
facts of Scripture in accordance with his theories."
In this sense, then, "the Bible is to the theologian
what nature is to the man of science."[28]

The point of Hodge's analogy between scientific
method and biblical interpretation is that the ultimate
criterion for judging theological claims is
faithfulness to scripture, just as the ultimate
criterion for judging scientific claims is faithfulness
to nature. His inductive method, then, has little or
nothing to do with natural theology, but is merely his
way of describing, in the scientific language of his
generation, the proper attitude of a biblical
theologian. The hallmark of that attitude is a
willingness to approach the text with as few
preconceptions as possible, and to modify or abandon
interpretations which do not hold up under continued
reading.

The Bible, properly interpreted, is thus the
primary source of knowledge about God. This does not
mean that it is the only source: the creation also
reveals God's being and attributes, as the Bible itself
attests; and Hodge affirms that "not only the being of
God, but also his eternal power and Godhead, are so
revealed in his works, as to lay a stable foundation
for natural theology." Nevertheless, "all that nature
teaches concerning God and our duties is more fully and
more authoritatively revealed in his Word;" and when it
comes to the justification of sinners before God,

"natural theology utterly fails." Only the Bible "contains all the facts or truths which form the contents of theology."[29]

In interpreting the Bible, the theologian relies to some extent on reason. According to Hodge, "revelation is the communication of truth to the mind," so reason is necessarily presupposed in every revelation. It is thus "the prerogative of reason to judge of the credibility of a revelation," at least in two respects. First, reason can determine whether an alleged revelation involves a contradiction, either with itself or with some other "well authenticated truth, whether of intuition, experience, or previous revelation;" if it does, it is logically impossible, and thus cannot be an object of faith. Second, reason can judge the evidence by which a revelation is supported; since by its very nature, faith "is not a blind, irrational assent, but an intelligent reception of the truth on adequate grounds," and even "the Scriptures never demand faith except on the ground of adequate evidence." Hodge cautions, however, against the extreme of rationalism, which he defines as "the system or theory which assigns undue authority to reason in matters of religion." The various forms of rationalism deny either the possibility, the necessity, or the actuality of divine revelation; and they assume instead that "the human intelligence is the measure of all truth." Hodge considers this "an insane presumption," since God is "infinite and of necessity incomprehensible." He distinguishes between knowledge and understanding: the former is "assent founded on the direct or indirect, the intuitive or discursive, apprehension of its object," whereas the latter entails thorough comprehension. Faith "implies knowledge," but "surely man may believe what he cannot understand." For example, everyone knows that like begets like; but "no man understands the mystery of reproduction." Furthermore, the doctrines of creation, fall, and redemption, "not depending on general principles of reason, but in great measure on the purposes of an intelligent, personal Being, can be known only so far as He chooses to reveal them." Scripture, and not reason, is thus the necessary and sufficient basis for faith.[30]

On the other hand, apprehension of scriptural truth is not an exercise of reason alone: it also requires the inward teaching of the Holy Spirit. Hodge affirms that "there is no form of conviction more intimate and irresistible than that which arises from the inward teaching of the Spirit;" which, however, is "confined to truths objectively revealed in the Scriptures." Hodge thus rejects mysticism, which he defines as the view that "the Spirit is given to every man as an inward teacher and guide, whose instructions and influence are the highest rule of faith, and sufficient, even without the Scriptures," to secure salvation. Although it is true that God can reveal truth directly to individuals, and on rare occasions has done so, and although it is true that the inward teaching of the Spirit is necessary for true faith, yet "it is plain that the Scriptures, and not an inward light common to all men, are, by the ordinance of God, the only source to us of saving and sanctifying knowledge." Furthermore, mysticism tends to make religious feelings the ground of faith, whereas in Hodge's view "the feelings come from spiritual

apprehension of the truth, and not the knowledge of
truth from the feelings." Mysticism exalts the
feelings, while rationalism exalts the reason; but both
err in shifting the basis of faith from the written
scriptures.[31]

Following the Reformers and the Westminster
Confession, then, Hodge considers the Bible "the only
infallible rule of faith and practice." This means
that "the Old and New Testaments are the Word of God,
written under the inspiration of the Holy Spirit, and
are therefore infallible, and of divine authority in
all things pertaining to faith and practice, and
consequently free from all error whether of doctrine,
fact, or precept." He also infers several "general
facts or principles which underlie the Bible, which are
assumed in its teachings, and which therefore must be
assumed in its interpretation." These include the fact
that God is "a Spirit, -- a self-conscious,
intelligent, voluntary agent;" that God is the extramundane creator of the world; that God is omnipresent
and "everywhere active, preserving and governing all
his creatures;" that although God "generally acts
according to fixed laws and through secondary causes,
He is free to act, and often does act immediately, or
without the intervention of such causes;" and, finally,
that "the Bible contains a divine, or supernatural
revelation."[32]

These facts being assumed, the question is what the
Bible teaches about the nature and effects of the
influence under which it was written. Hodge's answer
to this question is that "the common doctrine of the
Church is, and ever has been, that inspiration was an
influence of the Holy Spirit on the minds of certain

select men, which rendered them the organs of God for
the infallible communication of his mind and will.
They were in such a sense the organs of God, that what
they said God said." Hodge distinguishes this doctrine
of inspiration from "the mechanical theory" which
regards the sacred writers as mere machines. According
to Hodge, "the sacred writers impressed their
peculiarities on their several productions as plainly
as though they were the subjects of no extraordinary
influence," writing "out of the fulness of their own
thoughts and feelings" and employing "the language and
modes of expression which to them were the most natural
and appropriate." Nevertheless, Hodge insists, "they
spoke as they were moved by the Holy Ghost, and their
words were his words." This "doctrine of plenary
inspiration" is distinguished not only from mechanical
theories but also from "partial" theories which limit
inspiration either to certain books of the Bible, or to
the thoughts (but not the words) of the biblical
writers, or to the religious and moral teachings of
scripture. In contrast to these theories of partial
inspiration, Hodge maintains that "all the books of
Scripture were equally inspired. All alike are
infallible in what they teach." Furthermore, "the
thoughts are in the words. The two are inseparable."
Finally, inspiration "is not confined to moral or
religious truths, but extends to the statements of
facts, whether scientific, historical, or
geographical." In other words, plenary inspiration
"extends to everything which any sacred writer asserts
to be true."[33]

What, then, about the obvious objection that the
Bible actually contains contradictions and factual

errors? Hodge dismisses the contradictions as either
apparent or trivial, insisting that they "bear no
proportion to the whole. No sane man would deny that
the Parthenon was built of marble, even if here and
there a speck of sandstone should be detected in its
structure." With respect to errors in historical or
scientific facts, Hodge makes four points: (1) he
distinguishes "between what the sacred writers
themselves thought or believed, and what they teach,"
and he considers only the latter to be authoritative;
(2) he describes the language of the Bible as "the
language of common life," which is "founded on
apparent, and not upon scientific truth;" (3) he
repeats his distinction between facts and theories, and
maintains that the Bible may contradict the latter but
never the former; and (4) he distinguishes "between
the Bible and our interpretation," and acknowledges
that the latter is fallible. Thus, the Ptolemaic
theory that the sun moves around the earth may have
been held by the sacred writers, but it was not taught
by them. Furthermore, although for centuries the Bible
was interpreted in accordance with the Ptolemaic
theory, when the theory was shown to be false and the
Bible was reinterpreted accordingly, the Biblical
teachings were unaffected by the change.[34]

Hodge then turns from the method and source of
theology to theology proper. He begins with the origin
of the idea of God, proofs for the existence of God,
"anti-theism," and the extent to which God can be
known. Under the first topic, Hodge observes that all
people know that "there is a Being on whom they are
dependent, and to whom they are responsible." He
concludes that this rudimentary knowledge of God is

innate, by which he means that it is "due to our constitution, as sentient, rational, and moral beings," as opposed to founded on experience, reached by a process of reasoning, or derived exclusively from tradition. Hodge explains that he does <u>not</u> mean that people are born with innate ideas, but that "the mind is so constituted that it perceives certain things to be true without proof and without instruction." Knowledge of God is thus both universal and necessary, not in the sense that the nonexistence of God is absolutely unthinkable, but in the sense that God's existence, like "the existence of the external world, or the obligation of the moral law," cannot be denied "without doing violence to the laws of our nature."[35] The influence of Reid's common-sense philosophy is unmistakable here.

If knowledge of God's existence is innate, then why should it be desirable, or even possible, to prove it? Hodge defends the use of proofs for the existence of God on the grounds that "although all men have feelings and convictions which necessitate the assumption that there is a God," it is nevertheless "perfectly legitimate to show that there are other facts which necessarily lead to the same conclusion." Besides, such proofs are helpful in demonstrating that God is "a personal Being, self-conscious, intelligent, moral. All this may be inclosed in the primary intuition, but it needs to be brought out and established." The standard proofs are thus "not designed so much to prove the existence of an unknown being, as to demonstrate that the Being who reveals himself to man in the very constitution of his nature must be all that Theism declares him to be."[36]

Hodge then discusses four proofs for the existence of God: ontological, cosmological, teleological, and moral or anthropological. Of the four, the teleological receives by far the most emphasis, occupying about half of the discussion. Hodge first states the teleological argument in the form of a syllogism: "Design supposes a designer. The world everywhere exhibits marks of design. Therefore the world owes its existence to an intelligent author." For Hodge, the concept of design entails three things: "(1) The selection of an end to be attained. (2) The choice of suitable means for its attainment. (3) The actual application of those means for the accomplishment of the proposed end." This being the nature of design, it is self-evident that "design is indicative of intelligence, will, and power." Furthermore, the designer must be an external agent, because "the end, the thought, is prior to the product," even though, in distinction to human products, the works of nature "are fashioned as it were from within outward." Hodge then proceeds to list some of the evidence for design in nature: the eye and various other animal organs, the harmonious functioning of organs within an animal, the mutually beneficial relations between plants and animals, and so on. For additional examples, the reader is referred to the *Bridgewater Treatises* and Paley's *Natural Theology*.[37]

Hodge notes that the teleological argument is, of course, rejected by those who reject final causes; but he considers this to be merely another way of rejecting the existence of God: "The doctrine of final causes in nature must stand or fall with the doctrine of a personal God. The one cannot be denied without denying the other. And the admission of the one involves the admission of the other." Hodge also confronts the objections of Hume and Kant. To the objection that knowledge is limited by experience, and human beings have no experience of world-making, Hodge responds that the inference of an intelligent agent from evidence of design is not so much a conclusion from experience as it is "an intuitive truth, self-evident from its nature." To the objection that the teleological argument proves, at best, only a world-builder, and not an extramundane God, Hodge reiterates his claim that design must come from outside. Furthermore, since a cause must be adequate to its effect, and since the world is "incomprehensibly great" (which Hodge considers "practically equivalent" to being "infinitely great"), this extramundane designer must be infinitely great, and thus divine. Perhaps sensing the inadequacy of this response, Hodge suggests only that it "may be" sufficient; but in any case, he has no doubt that the teleological argument rules out the possibility that the universe could be due "either to chance, or the action of mere physical laws." Design must be the product of intelligence, and "not merely an unintelligent force acting according to necessary law."[38]

Hodge's next chapter is devoted to the refutation of various forms of "anti-theism," the most prominent of which is materialism. He defines materialism as "that system which ignores the distinction between matter and mind, and refers all the phenomena of the world, whether physical, vital, or mental, to the functions of matter." Natural scientists, in particular, are prone to adopt this view, which Hodge considers contrary to intuition, reason, experience, and scripture. Since reality transcends the material plane, the proponents of scientific materialism "are not entitled to claim the whole domain of knowledge as exclusively their own."[39]

Hodge then discusses the question of whether God can be known. He maintains that it is "the clear doctrine of the Scriptures that God can be known," though this does not mean that we can know all that is true concerning God. Our knowledge of God is partial and inadequate, but "nevertheless our knowledge, as far as it goes, is true knowledge. God really is what we believe Him to be, so far as our idea of Him is determined by the revelation which He has made of Himself in his works, in the constitution of our nature, in his word, and in the person of his Son." True knowledge, though not complete comprehension, is essential for faith, since it is impossible to believe in something which is totally unknown: "If, therefore, we cannot know God, we cannot believe in Him." Hodge compares this knowledge of God with knowledge of other persons: "How do we know that our nearest friend has a soul?" The soul is "mysterious and incomprehensible. Yet we know that it is, and what it is, just as certainly as we know that we ourselves are, and what we are. In the same way we know that God is, and what He is." Hodge considers this analogy valid because "we are the children of God, and, therefore, we are like Him." Nevertheless, the analogy is limited by the disturbing element of sin, which means that "reason and conscience are no longer adequate guides." Like Calvin, Hodge insists that the Bible is necessary for true knowledge of God.[40]

After dealing with God's attributes, the trinity, and predestination, Hodge turns to the doctrine of creation. The biblical doctrine is that "an extramundane God, existing out of, and before the world, absolutely independent of it," created all things out of nothing. This original creation was "instantaneous and immediate, i.e., without the intervention of any second causes;" but in addition to this immediate initial creation there is also "a mediate, progressive creation: the power of God working in union with second causes." It is possible that the phenomena of the vegetable and animal kingdoms are due to this gradual, mediate creation; but these phenomena could not be due to "the evolution of an unconscious, unintelligent force," which would be unable to proceed by design. That there is design in the creation is attested to by scripture, which teaches that "the glory of God, the manifestation of all his perfections, is the last end of all his works."[41]

God is not only the creator but also the preserver and governor of the world. God's providential government, according to Hodge, "includes the idea of design and control. It supposes an end to be attained, and the disposition and direction of means for its accomplishment." God "has some great end, including an indefinite number of subordinate ends," toward which the universe is directed. Hodge maintains that God's providential government is "universal, including all the creatures of God and all their actions." The doctrine of providence thereby "excludes both necessity and chance from the universe, substituting for them the intelligent and universal control of an infinite, omnipresent God." God's providential government is

also powerful, and thereby "renders certain the
accomplishment of his designs;" it is wise, and thus
"suited to the nature of the creatures over which it is
exercised," so that the material world is governed by
fixed laws, animals by instincts, and "rational
creatures agreeably to their nature;" and it is holy,
meaning that "there is nothing in the ends proposed,
the means adopted, or the agency employed," which is
inconsistent with God's holiness.[42]

Hodge considers the doctrine of God's providential
government "the foundation of all religion." It not
only "necessarily flows from the Scriptural idea of
God," but it can also be inferred from "the intelligent
adaptation of means to an end" which is "everywhere
manifest" in the creation and which is "evidence of
God's omnipresent intelligence and control." In
addition, the doctrine of providence is "demanded by
the religious nature of man," and "therefore an
instinctive and necessary belief;" and it is revealed
"to an intelligent eye" by "the history of the world."
Most conclusive, however, is the testimony of
scripture, which "asserts that the providential agency
of God is exercised over all the operations of nature,"
as well as over "nations and communities of men,"
though not in such a way as to make God the author of
sin.[43]

Hodge then contrasts the biblical doctrine of
providence with several other "theories of the divine
government:" the deistic view that after having created
the world and certain general laws God "leaves the
world to the guidance of those general laws;" the
"theory of entire dependence," held by some Christians,
which sees God as the only true cause and thus denies

the existence of secondary causes; the philosophical
doctrine that apart from mind there are no efficient
causes in the universe; and the Leibnizian theory of
preestablished harmony. Hodge also contrasts the
biblical doctrine with Turretin's scholastic doctrine
of concursus, objecting to the latter on the following
grounds: it arbitrarily and falsely denies that any
creature can originate actions it "is an attempt to
explain the inexplicable," since the mode of God's
action cannot be understood; and it multiplies
difficulties by raising "the most subtle and perplexing
metaphysical questions, which no man is able to solve."
Hodge prefers the simple affirmation that "God does
govern all his creatures" in a manner "consistent with
their nature, and with his own infinite purity and
excellence."[44]

This means, in most cases, that God acts through
secondary causes and the laws of nature. Although God
is the creator of the laws of nature, and thus
independent of them, "God never does disregard them
except for the accomplishment of some high purpose."
Since "the stability of the universe, and the welfare,
and even the existence of organized creatures, depend
on the uniformity of the laws of nature," God "in the
ordinary operations of his Providence, operates with
and through the laws which he has ordained." In other
words, God employs natural means just as human agents
do: physical forces, which otherwise would act by
necessity, blindly, and uniformly, are consciously and
intelligently directed toward an end. And just as the
human use of natural laws is consistent with their
uniformity, so "the control of God over them for the
accomplishment of his purposes cannot be inconsistent

with their stability." As an example of God's purposeful employment of natural laws, Hodge refers to the growth of an embryo. Since "matter cannot be made to do the work of mind," and "the whole animal body, with all its wonderful interdependencies and relations of parts and organs, and its designed adaptations for what is external and future," is "evidence of mind," God must be actively controlling secondary causes in vital processes such as reproduction and embryological development.[45]

On the other hand, Hodge follows the Westminster Confession in affirming that God is also "free to work without, above, or against" secondary causes. When God chooses to do so, the result is a miracle, which Hodge defines as "an event, in the external world, brought about by the immediate efficiency, or simple volition of God." Hodge defends not only the possibility but also the actuality of miracles, considering it "decisive" that "the Bible everywhere not only asserts the absolute independence of God of all his works, and his absolute control over them, but is also filled with examples of the actual exercise of this control." Hodge rejects the argument that what appear to be miracles are really just manifestations of higher laws of nature which have not yet been discovered. The assumption that there are such higher laws is a "gratuitous hypothesis" which is inconsistent with the fact that the Bible attributes miracles to the immediate power of God. Furthermore, "there are miracles which transcend not only all known, but all possible laws of nature. Nature cannot create. It cannot originate life; otherwise it would be God, and nothing beyond nature would be necessary to account for the universe."[46]

It is clear from the foregoing that Hodge is primarily a biblical theologian. Although he includes proofs for the existence of God in his *Systematic Theology*, and although he believes that God's existence can be known intuitively, at least in rudimentary outline, he has no doubt that the basic source of religious knowledge is scripture. Regardless of whether arguments based on other grounds seem conclusive or inconclusive, his ultimate recourse is to scripture. This applies as much to design as to every other doctrine. Common sense tells us that creation is designed, but the Bible tells us more directly, and in greater detail, exactly what is designed and why. God's existence can be inferred from design in nature, but it can be known with more certainty and clarity on the basis of scripture.

Hodge was thus convinced that the Bible is the most reliable source of religious knowledge. He was also convinced that the Bible, properly interpreted, could not conflict with the facts of nature, properly understood. His faith in the congruence of religious and natural knowledge was tested, of course, and not only by Darwinian evolution. Even before Darwin, Hodge was involved in controversies between religion and science; and before turning to his critique of Darwinism, it would be instructive to take a closer look at how Hodge applied his theology in those situations.

(4) Hodge and Science before Darwin

The profound confidence in the harmony of religion and science which Hodge inherited from his Presbyterian background was reflected in the *Biblical Repertory and Princeton Review*, which under Hodge's editorship affirmed that "there can be no contradiction between what God does and what he says." Or, as Hodge himself was fond of saying to his students, "the truth has nothing to fear from the truth." On the eve of the publication of Darwin's *Origin of Species*, Hodge wrote that "God in nature can never contradict God in the Bible and in the hearts of his people;" and even twelve years later, in the midst of the controversy over Darwinism, Hodge continued to insist that "there can be no conflict between the teachings of the Scriptures and the facts of science."[47]

This confidence in the harmony of religion and science enabled Hodge to defend, to some extent, the independence of science from religion. According to a July, 1851, "Short Notice" in the *Biblical Repertory and Princeton Review*, "because we are perfectly sure of ultimate agreement" between science and religion, "we are content to allow the devotees of the former to prosecute their researches and correct their deductions until this agreement is reached." In 1863, the *Biblical Repertory and Princeton Review* published an article by Joseph Clark on "The Skepticism of Science" which maintains that the church "has nothing to fear, but everything to expect, from the most extended researches and the most complete generalization of science;" and the church should thus "concede to science the largest possible liberty in her own sphere." Nearly a decade later, Volume I of Hodge's

Systematic Theology urges theologians to "let science take its course, assured that the Scriptures will accommodate themselves to all well authenticated scientific facts in time to come, as they have in time past."[48]

Implicit in the preceding remarks is the distinction between facts and theories with which Hodge begins his *Systematic Theology*. Facts and theories are both essential, and Hodge does not seem to have lapsed into the vulgar distortion of Baconianism which limits science to facts and denies it any explanatory function. An October, 1851, "Short Notice" in the *Biblical Repertory and Princeton Review* criticizes a book claiming that theoretical inductions transcend the legitimate limits of science. According to the "Short Notice," such a limitation would make true science impossible, since "science is not the simple knowledge and classification of phenomena, or 'facts,' but the knowledge and classification of the laws to which those phenomena are to be referred." Nevertheless, Hodge was thoroughly Baconian in giving facts priority over explanations. According to his *Systematic Theology*, the "fundamental principle of all sciences" is that "theory has to be determined by facts, and not facts by theory." Facts "do not admit of denial. They are determined by the wisdom and will of God. To deny facts, is to deny what God affirms to be true." Theories, on the other hand, "are human speculations, and can have no higher authority than their own inherent probability." Facts, being divine, cannot conflict with each other; but theories, being human, often do. Apparent discrepancies between scientific and religious truth arise only because scientists "are disposed to demand for their theories the authority due only to established facts;" while "theologians, because at liberty to reject theories, are sometimes led to assert their independence of facts."[49]

Both of these errors are to be avoided. On the one hand, to the extent that scientists go beyond facts in their inductions, they must recognize both the tentativeness of their theories and the importance of taking into account religious views on the same subject. According to Hodge, it is unreasonable as well as irreligious for scientists to "promulgate theories inconsistent with the facts of the Bible, when those theories are sustained by only plausible evidence, which does not command the assent even of the body of scientific men themselves." Generally speaking, moreover, any view which presumes to exclude the possibility of miracles, or God's direct intervention in the course of nature, is unacceptable. On the other hand, "it is unwise for theologians to insist on an interpretation of Scripture which brings it into collision with the facts of science." Since "theologians are not infallible," it may "happen in the future, as it has in the past, that interpretations of the Bible, long confidently received, must be modified or abandoned, to bring revelation into harmony with what God teaches in his works." This process "may be a painful trial to the Church, but it does not in the least impair the authority of the Scriptures. They remain infallible; we are merely convicted of having mistaken their meaning."[50]

The classic illustration of this latter point, and an example to which Hodge frequently refers, is the scriptural reinterpretation made necessary by the

Copernican revolution in astronomy: "So long as men
believed that the earth was the center of our system,
the sun its satellite, and the stars its ornamentation,
they of necessity understood the Bible in accordance
with that hypothesis. But when it was discovered that
the earth was only one of the smaller satellites of the
sun, and that the stars were worlds, then faith,
"although at first staggered, soon grew strong enough
to take it all in" as it realized that all along the
Bible had been "in full accord with these stupendous
revelations of science."[51] In other words, it was not
that scripture taught archaic science, but that archaic
science had been read into scripture by its
interpreters.

The reinterpretation of scripture under the impact
of Copernican astronomy had its parallel in Hodge's own
lifetime in the controversy over biblical chronology.
Until the rise of modern geological science in the
eighteenth and nineteenth centuries, the chronological
accuracy of the six days of creation in the first
chapter of Genesis, and the Old Testament genealogies
which seemed to fix the age of the earth at about six
thousand years, had been taken for granted. But as
geologists became more and more convinced that long
periods of time had intervened between the appearance
of various kinds of plants and animals, and that the
earth was much older than six thousand years,
Christians were faced with a choice of either rejecting
the conclusions of the geologists or re-interpreting
scriptural chronology. For those who chose the latter
alternative, the two most common options were the
British view (proposed by Chalmers) that the original
creation of the universe recorded in Genesis 1:1 was

followed by an indefinitely long interval before the
six days described in Genesis 1:3-2:2; and the French
view (supported by Buffon and Cuvier) that the six days
of Genesis represented six creative eras of indefinite
duration. The former, or "interval" theory, seemed
better suited to a literal interpretation of the
biblical text; but the latter, or "era" theory, seemed
more consistent with the fossil evidence.[52]

In the 1840's, Hodge (like most Americans)
preferred the interval theory. Under his editorship,
the *Biblical Repertory and Princeton Review* published
an 1841 article by M.B. Hope on "Scripture and
Geology," which concedes that scriptural re-
interpretation is necessary in the light of geological
evidence, just as it was in the face of Copernican
astronomy. The article rejects the era theory,
however, as philologically questionable and
scientifically unnecessary, and favors the interval
theory instead. During the same period, Hodge seems to
have taught only the interval theory in his lectures on
theology. According to lecture notes taken by one of
his students during the 1842-43 academic year, Hodge
was skeptical of the conclusions of geologists because
they seemed unable "to form any consistent, uniform,
universally admitted theory," and because they reached
their conclusions only by assuming "quite gratuitously"
that the rate of rock formation had always been
uniform. Nevertheless, the student's notes continue,
if geological findings were to necessitate scriptural
re-interpretation, "we do no force to the Mosaic
account by supposing the earth created many ages before
the six days' work of creation commenced." Lecture
notes in Hodge's own handwriting which seem to be from

the same decade also favor the interval theory: "Assuming the correctness of the conclusions of geologists, the most satisfactory mode of reconciliation of those conclusions with the Mosaic record is to regard the first verse of Genesis as declaring the general fact of a creation, and the following verses the last renovation of our globe preparatory to the creation of man."[53]

During the 1850's and 1860's, Hodge's thinking on this subject gradually changed, perhaps reflecting the increasing popularity of the era theory among Americans in general.[54] A student's notes of Hodge's lectures from the 1852-53 academic year repeat verbatim the 1840's version of the interval theory, and make no mention of the era theory. Four years later, however, notes by another student mention "the theory of the Eminent Christian Philosopher, Professor Guyot, of Princeton College," that the six days in the first chapter of Genesis "may each have been indefinite periods;" though the interval theory is still preferred as more consistent not only with scripture but also with "the different strata of the earth." In 1856, a book review appearing in the *Biblical Repertory and Princeton Review* declared that "if science should succeed in demonstrating that the earth is millions of years old, then we will with the utmost alacrity believe that the days of creation were periods of indefinite duration." A student's lecture notes from 1857 still consider the interval theory "the best answer" to the chronology problem; but notes taken by a student during the 1861-62 academic year seem to give approximately equal weight to the interval theory and the era theory.[55]

Throughout this period, Hodge differed from his more conservative contemporaries in remaining open to the possibility that scripture would have to be reinterpreted in the light of scientific evidence. For example, in 1863 the *New York Observer* attacked the *Biblical Repertory and Princeton Review* for maintaining that scientists should not be bound by biblical details in their investigations. According to the *Observer*, at issue was "the accuracy of the sacred record" of creation, which "took place about six thousand years ago; and the *Biblical Repertory and Princeton Review* was guilty of making "science lead the way and the Bible follow." Hodge's reply, which was published in the *Observer*, was that "nature is as truly a revelation of God as the Bible; and we only interpret the Word of God by the Word of God when we interpret the Bible by science." According to Hodge, Christians must avoid "a two-fold evil," neither formulating scientific theories which recklessly ignore scriptural truth, nor persisting in scriptural interpretations which conflict with well-established scientific truth. The *New York Observer* responded by reiterating its faith in biblical chronology: "We reject the so-called science of the naturalists, and accept as our highest authority in this scientific matter the records of holy men."[56]

Hodge obviously did not agree with the *New York Observer*. Although he never completely surrendered his skeptical attitude toward the conclusions of the geologists, he gradually changed his interpretation of scriptural chronology to make it more consistent with those conclusions. By 1871, Hodge had clearly abandoned the interval theory in favor of the era theory: Volume I of his *Systematic Theology* mentions

the former, but defends the latter as the best method
of reconciling the Mosaic account with the scientific
facts. Hodge notes that "the word day is used in
Scripture in many different senses," and he quotes
several examples to prove the point; he also cites two
prominent advocates of the era theory, James Dana of
Yale and Arnold Guyot of Princeton. But the most
persuasive argument in favor of the era theory is that
it provides the best fit between the Genesis account
and the scientific evidence. Since the ordinary sense
of "day" brings scripture "into conflict with facts,"
while the conflict can be avoided by interpreting the
word in the sense of "an indefinite period of time" (a
sense "which it undoubtedly has in other parts of
Scripture"), it is obligatory to adopt the era theory.
Once that theory is adopted, "there is not only no
discrepancy between the Mosaic account of the creation
and the assumed facts of geology, but there is a most
marvelous coincidence between them."[57]

Obviously, then, with respect to biblical
chronology Hodge was committed neither to a literal,
fundamentalist reading of the text nor to the more
conservative of the two most common alternative
interpretations. The actual development of his own
thinking from 1841 to 1871 shows that he was quite
capable of being persuaded by scientific evidence to
modify his interpretation of scripture. Thus when he
declared, at the semi-centennial celebration of his
Princeton Seminary professorship in 1872, that he was
"not afraid to say that a new idea never originated in
this Seminary," he did not mean he was opposed to all
new ideas. As long as a new idea was compatible with
Westminster Calvinism, and served to reconcile

scripture with established scientific facts, Hodge
would embrace it.[58]

On the other hand, Hodge was quite capable of
resisting a scientific theory if it was unsupported by
facts and contrary to scriptural truth. An excellent
example is his involvement in the nineteenth-century
controversy over the theory that the human races
constitute distinct species with separate origins.
Polygenism, as the theory was called, was a minority
view among the leading naturalists of the time, though
the eminent Louis Agassiz was among its supporters.
Polygenism had racist implications; but even more
fundamental, theologically, was its apparent denial of
the spiritual unity and universal sinfulness of
humankind. Hodge, like most of his American
contemporaries, believed that all the human races were
equally fallen (and at the same time equally eligible
for salvation) by virtue of having descended from one
fallen progenitor.[59]

According to Hodge, the advocates of polygenism
based their conclusions on insufficient data. Not only
did they fail to take into account the scientific
evidence which persuaded most of their colleagues of
the opposite conclusion, but they also ignored
scriptural "facts." In 1859 and 1862, Hodge wrote
articles for the *Biblical Repertory and Princeton
Review* criticizing the polygenists on both of these
grounds, marshalling the scientific evidence against
polygenism while arguing that scientists "should not
propound theories framed in view of scientific facts
alone, while they overlook the facts of religion."
These latter facts, "which, to say the least, are just
as certain, and infinitely more important" than the

former, include the "unity of species, and unity of origin" of the human races. The implication seems to be that when a choice between two competing theories cannot be made on the basis of conclusive scientific evidence, and when one theory is significantly more consistent with scripture than the other, the scriptural theory is to be preferred. When Hodge protested to the *New York Observer* in 1863 that the *Biblical Repertory and Princeton Review* was not guilty of subordinating scripture to science, he cited his position on polygenism to prove his point. Noting that the diversity of human races "may be accounted for by assuming different origins for the several races, or by the influence of climate and modes of life," Hodge concludes: "As the Bible asserts the historical, as well as the specific, unity of the race, there is an end to the question."[60]

By attributing the diversity of races to "the influence of climate and modes of life," Hodge was, in effect, advocating a limited theory of "development" (or, in modern terminology, "evolution"). He was not unique in this respect: the idea that the diversity of the human races results from development under differing environmental conditions was defended by many evangelical Protestants in early nineteenth-century America as the best alternative to polygenism. It was another matter entirely, however, to claim that one species could develop into another. In a footnote to his 1862 article criticizing polygenism, Hodge mentions Charles Darwin in print for the first time. According to Hodge, Darwin's theory is as far from polygenism as any theory could be, belonging "to the opposite pole of skeptical speculation in natural history." At one

extreme lay the diversity of origin of the human races,
and at the other extreme lay the unity of origin of
humans and monkeys.   Polygenism and Darwinism are thus
"mutually self destructive," and cannot endanger the
biblical view, which by comparison seems both
reasonable and moderate.[61]   Within a decade, however,
Hodge would be forced to take Darwinism much more
seriously.

NOTES

1. A.A. Hodge, *Life of Charles Hodge*, 13.

2. Ahlstrom, "Scottish Philosophy and American Theology," 261-265; Bozeman, *Protestants in an Age of Science*, 23-27, 30, 39-43; Daniels, *American Science in the Age of Jackson*, 6-7, 32-33, 191-200; Sloan, *Scottish Enlightenment and the American College Ideal*, 225-247.

3. A.A. Hodge, *Life of Charles Hodge*, 50-51. See also Hoffecker, *Piety and the Princeton Theologians*, 46. The Latin title of Turretin's work is used here, both because (to my knowledge) no English translation has been published and in order to distinguish it from Calvin's *Institutes of the Christian Religion*.

4. A.A. Hodge, *Life of Charles Hodge*, 247. See also Hoffecker, *Piety and the Princeton Theologians*, 49-50; A.A. Hodge, *Life of Charles Hodge*, 68-69, 94-95.

5. A.A. Hodge, *Life of Charles Hodge*, 247-257. See also the 1868 Index Volume of the *Biblical Repertory and Princeton Review*; Nelson, "Rise of the Princeton Theology," 289-301.

6. A.A.Hodge, *Life of Charles Hodge*, 323-324. Charles Hodge even began a commentary on Turretin's *Institutio*, a partial, handwritten rough draft of which is in the Speer Library, Princeton Theological Seminary, Princeton, New Jersey.

7. A.A. Hodge, *Life of Charles Hodge*, 453-459, 534-535. Charles Hodge's sermon notes are in the Speer Library, Princeton Theological Seminary, Princeton, New Jersey. See also Hoffecker, *Piety and the Princeton Theologians*, 44-47; Nelson, "Rise of the Princeton Theology," 315-320.

8. Wells, "The Stout and Persistent 'Theology' of Charles Hodge," 12.

9. Ahlstrom, "Scottish Philosophy and American Theology," 261-268; Ahlstrom, "Theology in America: A Historical Survey," 265; Bozeman, *Protestants in an Age of Science*, 5-7, 30.

10. Calvin, *Institutes*, bk. 1, ch. 7, sec. 1; bk. 3, ch. 2, sec. 6; bk. 4, ch. 8, sec. 8. See also Niesel, *Theology of Calvin*, 22-39; Wallace, *Calvin's Doctrine of the Word and Sacrament*, 97-114; Wendel, *Calvin*, 156-160.

11. Calvin, *Institutes*, bk. 1, ch. 2, sec. 1; bk. 1, ch. 5, sec. 1-2; bk. 1, ch. 6, sec. 1. See also Dowey, *Knowledge of God in Calvin's Theology*, 146-147, 221, 238-241; Klaaren, *Religious Origins of Modern Science*, 39-41; Niesel, *Theology of Calvin*, 41-53; Wendel, *Calvin*, 162-164.

12. Calvin, *Institutes*, bk. 1, ch. 16. See also Klaaren, *Religious Origins of Modern Science*, 42-44; Nelson, "Rise of the Princeton Theology," 6-8; Niesel, *Theology of Calvin*, 63-64, 70-72; Wendel, *Calvin*, 170, 177-180.

13. Schaff, *Creeds of Christendom*, 1:755-767, 3:600-613.

14. A. A. Hodge, *Life of Charles Hodge*, 13.

15. Schaff, *Creeds of Christendom*, 1:790-791.

16. Turretin, Institutio Theologiae Elencticae, topic 1, qq. 1, 3, 4, 8, 9. Quotations are from the incomplete handwritten translation by George Giger, one of Hodge's students, in the Speer Library, Princeton Theological Seminary, Princeton, New Jersey.

17. Turretin, *Institutio Theologiae Elencticae*, topic 2, q. 4, art. 3-5; topic 5, q. 4.

18. Schaff, *Creeds of Christendom*, 1:459. See also Beardslee, "Theological Development at Geneva," 364-372, 432-435; Schaff, *Creeds of Christendom*, 1:478-480.

19. Turretin, *Institutio Theologiae Elencticae*, topic 6, q. 1, art. 3. See also Beardslee, "Theological Development at Geneva," 169; *Encyclopedia of Religion and Ethics*, s.v. "Concursus"; Turretin, *Institutio Theologiae Elencticae*, topic 6, qq. 1-6.

20. Paley, *Natural Theology*, 329-330. See also Eiseley, *Darwin's Century*, 14-16, 174-178; Gillispie, *Genesis and Geology*, 19-20, 35-40, 104-106, 195-196, 209-219; Greene, *Death of Adam*, 1-10.

21. Bacon, *Works* 4:363-365 (*Advancement of Learning*,bk. 3). Commentators have pointed out that although Bacon's terminology for the four causes sounds Aristotelian, he means something rather different; for example, Bacon's "material cause" includes much of what Aristotle meant by formal as well as material cause. See Anderson, *The Philosophy of Francis Bacon*, 156-157; Copleston, *History of Philosophy*, vol. 3, pt. 2, 108.

22. Bacon, *Works*, 4:127 (*New Organon*, bk. 2). See also Anderson, *The Philosophy of Francis Bacon*, 185-186; Bozeman, *Protestants in an Age of Science*, 6, 16-17; Copleston, *History of Philosophy*, vol. 3, part 2, 114-121.

23. McCosh, *Scottish Philosophy*, 207-209; Grave, *Scottish Philosophy of Common Sense*, 114-136.

24. Lehrer and Beanblossom, eds., *Thomas Reid's Inquiry and Essays*, 20 (*Inquiry*, II:6). See also Grave, *Scottish Philosophy of Common Sense*, 114-134; Lehrer and Beanblossom, eds., *Thomas Reid's Inquiry and Essays*, xxv-xxx; McCosh, *Scottish Philosophy*, 159-160, 217-218, 221-224.

25. Kant, *Prolegomena to Any Future Metaphysics*, 7. See also Grave, *Scottish Philosophy of Common Sense*, 114-134.

26. Ahlstrom, "Scottish Philosophy and American Theology," 257-272; Bozeman, *Protestants in an Age of Science*, xv, 3-31, 162-164; Daniels, *American Science in the Age of Jackson*, 32-33, 63-85; Holifield, *Gentlemen Theologians*, 112-126; Sloan, *Scottish Enlightenment and the American College Ideal*, 225-247; Stewart, *Philosophical Essays*, xxviii-lxvi.

27. Charles Hodge, *Systematic Theology* 1:1-3, 18-19.

28. Hodge, *Systematic Theology* 1:3-15.

29. Hodge, *Systematic Theology* 1:17-28.

30. Hodge, *Systematic Theology* 1:4-6, 34-55.

31.   Hodge, *Systematic Theology* 1:6-9, 15, 61-103, 178-179.

32.   Hodge, *Systematic Theology* 1:104-154.

33.   Hodge, *Systematic Theology* 1:156-165, 181-182.

34.   Hodge, *Systematic Theology* 1:165-166, 169-171.

35.   Hodge, *Systematic Theology* 1:191-201.

36.   Hodge, *Systematic Theology* 1:202-203.

37.   Hodge, *Systematic Theology* 1:215-226.

38.   Hodge, *Systematic Theology* 1:227-230.

39.   Hodge, *Systematic Theology* 1:246-299.

40.   Hodge, *Systematic Theology* 1:335-365.

41.   Hodge, *Systematic Theology* 1:550-568.

42.   Hodge, *Systematic Theology* 1:575-582.

43.   Hodge, *Systematic Theology* 1:583-590.

44.   Hodge, *Systematic Theology* 1:591-605.

45.   Hodge, *Systematic Theology* 1:605-616.

46.   Hodge, *Systematic Theology* 1:617-625.

47.   Hope, "On the Relation between the Holy Scriptures and some parts of Geological Science," 391-392; Charles Hodge, Lecture Notes on "Creation," 12;   Hodge, "Unity of Mankind," 106-107;   Hodge, *Systematic Theology* 1:573. See also Bozeman, *Protestants in an Age of Science*, 39-41, 162-164.

48.   "Short Notices," 23 (1851): 556;   Clark, "Scepticism of Science," 65 (Hodge defends this article in "Bible in Science," 98-99); Hodge, *Systematic Theology* 1:57.

49.   Hodge, *Systematic Theology* 1:1; "Short Notices," 23 (1851): 696; Hodge, *Systematic Theology* 1:9-10, 13-14, 57-59, 276. See also Bozeman, *Protestants in an Age of Science*,162-164;

50. Hodge, *Systematic Theology* 1:56-59, 624. See also Eckard, "Logical Relations of Religion and Natural Science," 577-587; Hodge, "Unity of Mankind," 104-107.

51. Hodge, *Systematic Theology* 1:57, 171, 569-574.

52. Gillispie, *Genesis and Geology*, 52-65, 106, 178, 224-225; Millhauser, "Scriptural Geologists," 68-70.

53. Hope, "On the Relation between the Holy Scriptures and some parts of Geological Science," 384-385; Hodge, Lecture Notes on "Creation," 12; Student's Notes of Lectures, 1842-1843.

54. Millhauser, "Scriptural Geologists," 79-81.

55. Casper Hodge and Classmate, Notes of Lectures, 1852-1853; Harlow, Notes of Lectures, 1856-1857; "Short Notices," 28 (1856): 161-163; Farnham, Notes of Lectures, 1857; Baker, Notes of Lectures, 1861-1862. In 1862, Hodge, like Turretin, was willing to speculate that the initial creation of the world took place "near the autumnal equinox," a speculation that he omitted from his *Systematic Theology* a decade later (see Charles Hodge, "Diversity of Species in the Human Race," 463).

56. Clark, "Scepticism of Science," 56-58; "Scripture and Science," 82; Charles Hodge, "Bible in Science," 98-99.

57. Charles Hodge, *Systematic Theology* 1:570-574.

58. Hodge, "Address," 52. See also Ahlstrom, "Theology in America," 264.

59. Bowler, *Evolution: History of an Idea*, 282, 290-299; Bozeman, *Protestants in an Age of Science*, 109-111; Greene, *Death of Adam*, 221-247, 316-319, 327.

60. Charles Hodge, "Unity of Mankind," 104-108; Hodge, "Diversity of Species in the Human Race," 462-464; Hodge, "Bible in Science," 99. Hodge's position on polygenism remained essentially unchanged after the publication of these articles, and was reiterated in his *Systematic Theology*, 1:56-57, 2:77-91.

61. Hodge, "Bible in Science," 99; Hodge, "Diversity of Species in the Human Race," 461n. See also Clark, "Scepticism of Science," 43-75; Hovenkamp, *Science and*

Religion in America, 188-189; Student's Notes of
Lectures, 1842-1843.

CHAPTER THREE
The Critique: Hodge Versus Darwinism

Although Hodge made some brief references to Darwin
and evolution in earlier writings, his critique of
Darwinism is largely confined to three published
sources: Volume II of his *Systematic Theology*,
published in 1872; an impromptu debate on Darwinism at
the New York Conference of the Evangelical Alliance in
1873; and *What Is Darwinism*?, published in 1874. This
chapter begins by summarizing the relevant contents of
these sources and showing how Hodge sharpened his focus
in some ways during the controversy; and it concludes
with a critical analysis which distinguishes some non-
theological and theologically peripheral issues from
those more central to Hodge's mature position.

(1) Systematic Theology II (1872)
Hodge had previously criticized "development" as a
false theory of the "creation of man," and he now
locates his critique of Darwinism in the Anthropology
section of *Systematic Theology*. Volume II, published
in 1872, begins with a brief statement of the
"scriptural doctrine" of human origins. Quoting
Genesis 1 and 2, Hodge concludes that the doctrine
contains two elements: (1) that "man's body was formed
by the immediate intervention of God. It did not grow;
nor was it produced by any process of development."

Furthermore, (2) "the soul was derived from God."
Hodge then proceeds to examine various "anti-scriptural
theories" of human origins, beginning with spontaneous
generation and the development theories of Lamarck and
the author of *Vestiges of Creation*.[1]

Turning to Darwin, Hodge acknowledges that "he
stands in the first rank of naturalists, and is on all
sides respected not only for his knowledge and his
skill in observation and description, but for his
frankness and fairness." Hodge points out that "Darwin
differs from his predecessors" in that "he starts with
life, they with dead matter;" he "refers the origin of
species mainly to the laws of nature operating ab
extra" (by killing the weak and preserving the strong),
whereas earlier theories had relied on some "inward
process of development;" and he holds that new species
"arise by a slow process of very minute changes,"
whereas the author of *Vestiges of Creation* had supposed
them to be formed suddenly. All of the theories,
however, suffer from the same basic defect: they all
refer "the infinite diversities and marvellous
organisms of plants and animals" to "the operation of
unintelligent physical causes."[2]

Hodge proceeds to summarize the basic principles of
the Darwinian theory, which include: (1) the "law of
heredity," that like begets like; (2) the "law of
variation," that while offspring are essentially like
their parents they always differ from them "more or
less" in ways which may be deleterious, indifferent, or
advantageous; (3) the "struggle for life," arising from
the tendency of populations to increase more rapidly
than their means of support; and (4) "natural
selection," or survival of the fittest, which, "without

intelligence or purpose, selects the individuals best
adapted to continue and improve the race."3

Having thus outlined Darwin's theory and
distinguished it from its predecessors, Hodge begins
his critique with four "remarks:" First, the theory
"shocks the common sense of unsophisticated men," and
would probably not be taken seriously if it were not
for the "the spirit of the age" and "the real learning
of its author and advocates."[4]

Second, the theory "cannot be true" because it
"assumes that matter does the work of mind." This
"absurdity" is unacceptable to everyone except
materialists. Not only does Darwin attribute "the
infinite variety of vegetable and animal organisms" to
mere natural causes, but he also "argues against the
intervention of mind anywhere in the process."[5]

Third, the theory "is thoroughly atheistic, and
therefore cannot possibly stand." This is not to say
that Darwin himself is an atheist, since he "expressly
acknowledges the existence of God." In fact, Hodge
believes that "there may be a theistic interpretation
of the Darwinian theory," and cites the theistic
evolutionism of the Duke of Argyll as an example.
Referring to Asa Gray's defense of Darwinism, however,
Hodge concludes that such arguments "only go to prove
that the doctrine of development, or derivation of
species, may be held in a form consistent with theism.
This no one denies. They do not prove that Mr. Darwin
presents it in that form." According to Hodge, Darwin
does not interpret evolution in a theistic sense,
because for Darwin God's activity ended after creating
the first living germ or germs. Since that time,
according to Hodge's reading of the theory, "God has no

more to do with the universe than if He did not exist."
Furthermore, Darwin "obliterates all the evidences of
the being of God in the world" by attributing to
"physical causes" features of living organisms which
"all theists believe to be due to the operations of the
Divine mind." This amounts to atheism, because there
is "no more effectual way of getting rid of a truth
than by rejecting the proofs on which it rests." Hodge
enlists the opinions of Huxley, Buchner and Wallace to
support his charge that Darwinism excludes design.
Quoting Gray's statement that "the proposition that
things and events in nature were not designed to be so,
if logically carried out, is doubtless tantamount to
atheism," Hodge concludes that Darwin "does teach
precisely what Dr. Gray pronounces atheism."[6]

Fourth, Hodge remarks that Darwin's theory "is a
mere hypothesis, from its nature incapable of proof."
It cannot be proved because it attempts to explain not
only the origin of species, but also of "mental and
moral powers," in terms of physical causes, whereas
"what concerns the origin of things cannot be known
except by supernatural revelation."[7]

Hodge then summarizes seven different "theories of
the universe:" (1) the "purely atheistic theory" of
extreme materialism: (2) the theories of Lamarck and
the author of *Vestiges of Creation*, which admit an
initial "creation of matter," but deny "any further
intervention of God in the world," and refer the origin
of life to physical causes; (3) Darwin's theory, which
is like (2) except that it admits the creation not only
of matter but also of one or a few primordial living
germs, and it completely excludes teleology by
attributing organic diversity to "unintelligent natural

causes, and accidental variations;" (4) theories which grant the necessity of intelligence, but "place this intelligence in nature and not in God;" (5) Owen's theory, which attributes evolution to "inherent tendencies" in organisms which fulfill a pre-ordained divine plan;(6) the "reign of law" theory, which sees the necessity of intelligent design and locates intelligence in God, but repudiates the supernatural, since it "does not admit that God ever works except through second causes or by the laws of nature;" and, finally, (7) the "Scriptural doctrine."[8]

According to Hodge, the "Scriptural doctrine" teaches three things: (1) that "matter is not eternal, nor is life self-originating," but that "the universe and all it contains owe their existence to the will and power of God;" (2) that God "endowed matter with properties or forces," through which "He works in all the ordinary operations of his providence," using them "everywhere and constantly, as we use them in our narrow sphere;" and (3) that in the beginning God "created, or caused to be, every distinct kind of plant and animal." Hodge interprets the doctrine to mean that "each species was specially created, not ex nihilo, or without the intervention of secondary causes, but nevertheless originally, or not derived, evolved, or developed from pre-existing species." He distinguishes, however, between two kinds of species, "natural" and "artificial": the former "have their foundation in nature," have "a distinct origin," and "are capable of indefinite propagation;" while the latter "are such distinctions as naturalists have made for their own convenience," and are thus "simply varieties." Furthermore, by "originally created"

Hodge does not mean created simultaneously with the origin of the universe; instead, he means that new species which appear subsequent to the initial creation "owe their existence to the immediate intervention of God."[9]

Hodge protests that Darwinism is a mere "arraying of probabilities" against these "clear teachings of Scripture." He acknowledges, however, that "one of the great excellencies of Mr. Darwin is his candor," since he admits "that there are grave objections against the doctrine which he endeavors to establish." Hodge then lists some of the admitted objections, including the absence of connecting fossil links, the fact that species transitions have not been observed, the difficulty of believing that complex organs and instincts have developed without intelligent design, the sterility of hybrids, and the geographic distribution of species. Still another objection to Darwinism, according to Hodge, is the immutability of species. Citing Cuvier and Agassiz (among others) as authorities on this point, Hodge concludes that since species are immutable, their existence "must be due to the agency of God, mediate or immediate, and in either case so exercised as to make them answer a thought or purpose in the divine mind." In particular, "man does not owe his origin to the gradual development of a lower form of irrational life, but to the energy of his Maker." Finally, Hodge rejects Darwin's "pan-genesis" theory of heredity, since "reproduction, as involving the control of physical causes to accomplish a purpose, is a work of intelligence;" and it would be "far easier to believe in fairies" than to believe that Darwin's "gem-mules" are "seats of intelligence."[10]

Scientific objections to Darwinism, according to Hodge, bring satisfaction to "ordinary men," who "reject this Darwinian theory with indignation as well as with decision, not only because it calls upon them to accept the possible as demonstrably true, but because it ascribes to blind, unintelligent causes the wonders of purpose and design which the world everywhere exhibits; and because it effectually banishes God from his works."[11]

In addition to criticizing Darwinism, Volume II of *Systematic Theology* also deals with several related subjects. One is biblical chronology: although Hodge doubts that mankind is as old as some naturalists claim, he reiterates his view that the Bible was <u>not</u> intended to teach a literal chronology. The "Scriptures do not teach us how long men have existed on the earth. Their tables of genealogy were intended to prove that Christ was the son of David and of the seed of Abraham, and not how many years had elapsed between the creation and the advent."[12]

A second related topic is the fall of Adam. In addition to arguing (as he had for decades) that the human races all constitute one species with a common origin, Hodge cites "the direct testimony of the Scriptures" to show that "all men are the descendants of one fallen progenitor," and that "man was originally created in a state of maturity and perfection." Hodge interprets this to mean that "the primitive state of our race was not one of barbarism from which men have raised themselves by a slow process of improvement." This last point could be construed as an objection to Darwinism, though Hodge does not identify it as such.[13]

(2) Conference of the Evangelical Alliance (1873)

While Hodge was expanding his treatment of
Darwinism in *Systematic Theology* to the finished
critique he would present in *What Is Darwinism?*, he
attended the 1873 meeting of the Evangelical Alliance
in New York. A Protestant ecumenical organization
later superseded in America by the National Council of
Churches, the Evangelical Alliance had brought together
about a hundred men from various countries and various
disciplines to discuss the "important theological,
religious, and moral questions of the age." One of
those questions was evolution.[14]

On October 6, 1873, the fourth day of the
Conference, Rev. James McCosh of the College of New
Jersey led off with a paper on "Religious Aspects of
the Doctrine of Development." McCosh argued that
"development or evolution" is "merely an exhibition of
order running through successive ages." The actual
duration of the ages is not a matter of concern for
religion, because scripture "contains no inspired
chronology of early history." Furthermore, it is "for
scientific men to settle" the question of which powers
in nature may contribute to an "advance from age to age
from lower to higher forms." McCosh cautioned,
however, that "we can not, apart from a designing mind,
account for that combination, that organization of
agencies" which "produces development." Intelligent
thought, especially, could not have emerged from
matter, and McCosh felt that Darwin's theory was "weak"
on this point. Nevertheless, McCosh was confident of
the essential "correspondence" between the scriptural
view and the scientific view: "It is the same world,
seen under different aspects."[15]

When McCosh finished, Rev. G.W. Weldon of London remarked that, in deciding whether or not to accept the "theory of the amiable, but I think mistaken, Professor Darwin," it is important to recognize that scripture "was not intended to instruct us in science or the details of history," but rather "to teach man the way of access to God through Jesus Christ." Following Weldon's remarks, Rev. J.C. Brown of England confessed that he found no conflict between "the hypothesis of development" and the Westminister Catechism; on the contrary, he was convinced that general acceptance of the hypothesis would "ultimately exercise a beneficial influence on religion."[16]

Apparently this was too much for Hodge, and he rose to speak. According to one observer, he was "the most impressive personality of the Alliance," a picture of "strength lying in repose," with a face both "radiant" and "serene." But Hodge was also in his seventy-sixth year; and the same observer noted that, carrying "a gold-headed ebony cane, upon the top of which he is wont to recline, he is growing old far too fast. When he addresses the audience only those who are halfway toward the platform can have any pleasure in hearing."[17]

Hodge got right to the point: "I rise simply to ask Dr. Brown one question. I want him to tell us what development is. That has not been done. The great question which divides theists from atheists -- Christians from unbelievers -- is this: Is development an intellectual process guided by God, or is it a blind process of unintelligible [sic], unconscious force, which knows no end and adopts no means? In other words, is God the author of all we see, the creator of

all the beauty and grandeur of this world, or is
unintelligible force, gravity, electricity, and such
like?"[18]

Brown answered that what he understood by the
development hypothesis was that "not only what we call
species, but what many call genera and orders" are
"modified developments of the same formation;" and he
affirmed his belief "that everything in heaven and
earth and hell was created by the Lord and Father of
our Saviour Jesus Christ." This did not settle the
issue, of course, since Brown did not clarify whether
he thought the Lord actively guided the process of
development or left it to the operation of "unconscious
force." Further discussion, however, was postponed
until later in the day.[19]

Several more papers were read, including one by
Princeton geologist A.H. Guyot which interpreted
Genesis chronology in terms of "cosmogonic days" of
indefinite duration, and one by Principal J.W. Dawson
of McGill College in Montreal which attempted to
harmonize recent archaeological discoveries with
scripture. After the last paper of the day, the
discussion of evolution was reopened. One participant
asked Dawson "whether there is any necessary antagonism
between the Darwinian system and the Christian
religion." Dawson replied that it would "require a
treatise" to answer the question, and he scarcely knew
where to begin. He said that Darwinism is "only one
branch" of the materialistic speculations exemplified
by the doctrine of evolution held by Spencer, and that
it was not based on adequate scientific evidence; but
he recommended the whole issue as worthy of study.[20]

Hodge was not satisfied with Dawson's response, and he again rose to speak: "My idea of Darwinism is that it teaches that all the forms of vegetable and animal life, including man and all the organs of the human body, are the result of unintelligent, undesignating [sic] forces; and that the human eye was formed by mere unconscious action. Now, according to my idea, that is a denial of what the Bible teaches, of what reason teaches, and of what the conscience of any human being teaches; for it is impossible for any such organ as the eye to be formed by blind forces. It excludes God; it excludes intelligence from every thing. Am I right?"[21]

Dawson responded that Darwin himself would probably "not admit so much," but that "his doctrine logically leads to that conclusion." Dawson felt that Darwin's theory conflicts with the Bible, "especially with respect to man," and that it is not a result of scientific induction but a merely hypothetical alternative to the doctrine of creation. President M.B. Anderson of Rochester University concluded the debate by distinguishing between two meanings of evolution: a name for "the process of the Almighty in developing the plan of creation;" and a name for "the process of growth of the universe, discounting from the word all reference to volition, or pre-existing, consciously formed plan or idea."[22]

(3) What Is Darwinism? (1874)

"What is Darwinism? This is a question which needs an answer." Because of the "great confusion and diversity of opinion," some people consider Darwinism to be virtually atheistic, while others see it as "some harmless form of the doctrine of evolution." Hodge

thus begins by distinguishing Darwinism in particular
from evolution in general. He then sets himself the
task of explaining Darwin's theory before discussing
its merits.[23] Although much of what follows bears an
obvious resemblance to the material in *Systematic
Theology*, the various themes are reworded, rearranged,
and given different emphases.

Since Darwinism is a theory of the universe which
attempts to account for the origin of living things,
Hodge considers it appropriate to state first "the
other prevalent theories on this great subject" for the
purpose of comparison. He begins with "the scriptural
solution to the problem." The universe owes its
existence to the will of God, who is "spirit," and
therefore "a person," a "self-conscious, intelligent,
voluntary agent." God not only created the universe,
but also "controls all physical causes, working through
them, with them, and without them, as He sees fit."
Just as we purposefully use physical causes to
accomplish our ends, so "God everywhere and always
cooperates with them to accomplish his infinitely wise
and merciful designs." Furthermore, the human body is
"a part of the universe," but the human soul is a
spirit, and therefore "God-like." According to Hodge,
the truth of this doctrine "rests not only on the
authority of the Scriptures, but on the very
constitution of our nature," being "inscribed
ineffaceably" on "the heart of every human being."[24]

Hodge goes on to describe pantheism, Epicurean
atomism, Spencerian evolutionism, and hylozoism,
pointing out how each one differs from the scriptural
solution. He then examines "theism in unscriptural
forms," by which he means, on the one hand, admitting

God as the initial creator but attributing all subsequent events to natural causes operating without God's direct guidance, and on the other hand, denying the existence of natural causes altogether and attributing everything directly to God's agency. Having thus set the stage, Hodge proceeds to a description of "Mr. Darwin's theory."[25]

Hodge acknowledges that, unlike Spencer's works, the *Origin of Species* does "not purport to be philosophical." Hodge describes Darwin as "simply a naturalist, a careful and laborious observer," who is "singularly candid in dealing with the difficulties" of his theory. The problem which he sets for himself is to account for the fauna and flora of the earth. In attempting to solve this problem, Darwin makes, according to Hodge, certain assumptions: the reality of matter, the efficacy of physical causes, the existence of a creator (though without assuming anything further about the relation between the creator and the world), and the "existence of life in the form of one or more primordial germs," from which all living organisms have descended.[26]

Hodge then summarizes, somewhat more fully than he did in *Systematic Theology*, the natural laws which comprise Darwin's theory. These include: (1) the law of Heredity; (2) the law of Variation; (3) the law of Over Production, leading to a "struggle for life;" and (4) the law of Natural Selection, or Survival of the Fittest, which, given sufficient time, may produce "very gradually, great changes of structure," leading to the production of "not only species, but genera, families and orders in the vegetable and animal world." Hodge quotes extensively from the *Origin of Species* to illustrate what Darwin means by natural selection; and he quotes from *The Descent of Man* to show that Darwin intends to explain not only the origin of species in general, but also the origin of human beings, including mental faculties, moral nature, and religious sentiments.[27]

Proceeding to "the heart of Mr. Darwin's theory," Hodge asserts that "the main idea of his system lies in the word 'natural'." According to Hodge, Darwin uses the word in two senses: as antithetical to "artificial" (as in domestic breeding), and as antithetical to "supernatural," by which "Mr. Darwin intends to exclude design." In other words, natural selection involves "the operation of natural laws" but excludes intelligent purpose. Hodge distinguishes this both from the scriptural view and the deistic view: according to the former, the "innumerable instances of at least apparent contrivance" in living things are due to God's purposeful guidance of physical causes; and according to the latter, even though physical causes are autonomous God at least "endowed matter with forces which He foresaw and intended should produce" the contrivances which we see. By contrast, Darwin's view attributes them solely "to the blind operation of natural causes." This, according to Hodge, is materialism; and "to this doctrine, we are sorry to say, Mr. Darwin, although himself a theist, has given his adhesion." Hodge then points out that the idea of evolution is not new with Darwin, and that a person "may be an evolutionist without being a Darwinian." Even the idea of natural selection antedates Darwin, so "the peculiar character and importance" of Darwin's theory is that it uses natural selection in such a way

as to exclude all teleology. More precisely, "it is
the distinctive doctrine of Mr. Darwin, that species
owe their origin, not to the original intention of the
divine mind; not to special acts of creation calling
new forms into existence at certain epochs; not to the
constant and everywhere operative efficiency of God,
guiding physical causes in the production of intended
effects; but to the gradual accumulation of unintended
variations of structure and instinct, securing some
advantage to their subjects."[28]

To prove that his characterization of Darwinism is
correct, Hodge cites several paragraphs of "Darwin's
own testimony" from the *Origin of Species* and *The
Variation of Animals and Plants Under Domestication*.
These books are interpreted as asserting "that all the
organs of plants and animals, all their instincts and
mental endowments, may be accounted for by the blind
operation of natural causes, without any intention,
purpose, or cooperation of God." Hodge then quotes
extensively from advocates of the theory (Wallace,
Huxley, Bucher, Vogt, and Haeckel), and from opponents
of the theory (Argyll, Agassiz, Janet, Flourens,
Mitchell and Dawson), concluding that "as the advocates
of Mr. Darwin's theory defend and applaud it because it
excludes design, and as its opponents make that the
main ground of their objection to it, there can be no
reasonable doubt as to its real character."[29]

In a digression on the relation between science and
religion, Hodge notes that "there is an antagonism
between scientific men as a class, and religious men as
a class," though this antagonism "is neither felt nor
expressed by all on either side." He attributes the
conflict to three causes: (1) natural science credits

only "phenomena which we recognize through the senses,"
while religion rests on "intuitions of the reason and
the conscience" and "the grace of God;" (2) many
people fail to distinguish between facts and
explanations, the former being "from God" and therefore
unchanging, and the latter "from men" and therefore
mutable; and (3) those scientists who are hostile to
religion tend to adopt an attitude of superiority, even
contempt, for "the men of culture who do not belong to
their own class." According to Hodge, Huxley's advice
to theologians "to let science alone" will not resolve
the conflict, because "no department of human knowledge
is isolated," and because scientists "not only
speculate, but dogmatize, on the highest questions of
philosophy, morality, and religion." Nor is the
conflict to be resolved by saying that religion is
merely a matter of feeling, since "religion is a system
of knowledge, as well as a state of feeling." Harmony
between science and religion will come only when
"scientific men" recognize that "there are other kinds
of evidence of truth than the testimony of the senses,"
and learn to respect those who rely on such evidence.[30]

Returning to his main theme, Hodge reiterates his
acknowledgement that a person "may be an evolutionist
and yet not be an atheist and may admit of design in
nature." But Hodge "cannot see how the theory of
evolution can be reconciled with declarations of the
Scriptures." Without elaborating, he goes on to say
that Darwin's theory also suffers from the following
additional objections: (1) it is prima facie
incredible to suppose that all forms of life have
evolved from one primordial germ; (2) the theory
cannot be proved, but is merely "possible," as Darwin

himself admits; (3) the scientific facts have not changed since *Vestiges of Creation* was "universally rejected" thirty years before, and the only new factor appears to be Darwin's exclusion of design; and (4) the evidence indicating that species are immutable militates "not only against Darwinism, but against evolution in all its forms."[31]

Asserting that it is "a fixed law of nature" that "new species cannot be produced," Hodge then tackles the definition of "species" and concedes that this is "a question which it is exceedingly difficult to answer." He begins by distinguishing between mere species and true "primordial forms," granting that "no man asserts the immutability of all those varieties of plants and animals, which naturalists, for the convenience of classification, may call distinct species." Only primordial forms are immutable, and the criteria for distinguishing them are morphology, physiology, and "permanent fecundity" (by which Hodge means to exclude hybrids). As evidence for the immutability of "true" species, Hodge notes that they are known to have existed unchanged for very long periods of time, and that every true species first appears in its fully developed form without transitional links connecting it to other species. The unbridgeable gaps between species, like the gaps between dead and living matter, between plants and animals, and between animal instinct and the human mind, are stumbling-blocks to any theory of evolution. Another stumbling-block is heredity, which is "in its nature in the highest degree teleological," since it implies "determination of something future."[32]

Summing up, Hodge reiterates what he takes to be
the salient feature of Darwinian evolution: "All the
innumerable varieties of plants, all the countless
forms of animals, with all their instincts and
faculties, all the varieties of man with their
intellectual endowments, and their moral and religious
nature, have, according to Darwin, been evolved by the
agency of the blind, unconscious laws of nature."
Defining design to mean "the intelligent and voluntary
selection of an end, and the intelligent and voluntary
choice, application, and control of means appropriate
to the accomplishment of that end," Hodge concludes
that the "grand and fatal objection to Darwinism" is
its "exclusion of design in the origin of species."
Hodge then quotes (as he did in *Systematic Theology*)
Asa Gray's dictum that a denial of design in nature
would be "tantamount to atheism." Although Gray
thought Darwinism did not deny design, Hodge points out
that Darwin himself disagreed with Gray on this point,
and therefore that Gray's dictum is, in fact,
applicable to Darwinism: "We have thus arrived at the
answer to our question, What is Darwinism? It is
Atheism."[33]

(4) Analysis of the Argument

Darwinism is atheism. A simple conclusion to a
not-so-simple argument. Not only does Hodge find many
different kinds of reasons for objecting to Darwinism,
some obviously more plausible than others, but he also
varies the emphasis he places on those reasons over the
course of the controversy. Furthermore, the logic of
Hodge's argument, to say the least, is not always
clear. The purpose of the following analysis is to

distinguish non-theological objections from theological
ones, and among the latter to distinguish peripheral
issues from those more central to Hodge's mature
position. The analysis also attempts to clarify the
logic of Hodge's argument, in order to discover what he
took to be the root of the conflict between Darwinism
and Christianity.

Before proceeding with the analysis, however, two
preliminary observations are in order. First, Hodge
frequently makes a point of distinguishing between
Darwin's theory and Darwin himself. In fact, while
criticizing the theory he often praises Darwin for his
excellence as a naturalist, and for his fairness and
candor. This accords well with Hodge's own fundamental
rules for polemic theology, which state that the motive
of polemics "should be love of truth," and therefore
that personalities should be avoided lest the
controversy sacrifice "the very essence of
Christianity." Furthermore, although it is justifiable
to show the error of a position by tracing consequences
which follow from it, "we ought not to charge the
person embracing it with holding these consequences."
In keeping with this principle, Hodge repeatedly
cautions that although he finds Darwin's theory
atheistic, he is not attributing atheism to Darwin
himself.[34]

Second, Hodge's rules for polemic theology demand
"that the state of the controversy should be clearly
understood." He therefore endeavors to acquaint
himself with the "whole system" of his opponent, and to
avoid misrepresenting it in the debate. Accordingly,
Hodge read no less than three of Darwin's works, the
Origin of Species, *The Descent of Man*, and *The*

Variation of Animals and Plants Under Domestication,
and he quotes extensively from all three in the course
of his critique. Hodge represents Darwin's system in
terms of four principles or laws: Heredity; Variation;
Over-Production leading to a Struggle for Life; and
Natural Selection, or Survival of the Fittest.
Darwin's version in the *Origin of Species* actually
reads: Growth with Reproduction; Inheritance "which is
almost implied by reproduction;" Variability; and "a
Ratio of Increase so high as to lead to a Struggle for
Life, and as a consequence to Natural Selection,
entailing Divergence of Character and the Extinction of
less-improved forms." Although Hodge combines
inheritance and reproduction, the differences between
the two lists are minor; and it seems fair to say that
although someone like Asa Gray might disagree with the
consequences Hodge deduces from Darwin's theory, he
represents the theory itself with reasonable
accuracy.[35]

Hodge's non-theological reasons for objecting to
Darwinism may be roughly divided into (1) scientific
and (2) philosophical/psychological objections (though
one issue, the immutability of species, will appear in
both lists, as well as in the list of theological
objections). The scientific objections, which Hodge
merely borrows from his scientific contemporaries,
include the absence of connecting fossil links, the
sterility of hybrids, and the fact that species
transitions have never been observed. The professional
conclusion of some naturalists (such as Cuvier and
Agassiz) that species are therefore immutable could
also be considered a scientific objection. In Hodge's
critique, these objections serve the following

function: if Darwinism and Christianity are contradictory, then they cannot both be true; but if Darwinism can be shown to be false, then it is still possible for Christianity to be true. The present analysis, however, is not concerned with the truth or falsity of either Darwinism or Christianity, but merely with Hodge's view of the theological conflict between them. Therefore, Hodge's scientific objections to Darwinism, having been duly noted, may be ignored for the remainder of this discussion.

Hodge's philosophical/psychological objections include his claims that Darwinism is incredible because it shocks the common sense, absurd because matter cannot do the work of mind, incapable of being proved because a mere hypothesis, impossible because true species are by definition immutable, difficult to believe because organs seem to be designed, covertly teleological because vital processes like heredity already imply goal-directed activity, and currently in vogue not because of scientific evidence but only because the "spirit of the age" favors a rejection of design. Some of these objections function in a way similar to Hodge's scientific objections, providing grounds for concluding that Darwinism cannot be true; while others provide grounds for the somewhat milder conclusion that Darwinism could never be more than a mere "possibility" and thus no real threat to the truth of Christianity. Many of them are clearly conditioned by the Scottish common-sense philosophy and Baconian inductivism which Hodge shared with many of his American contemporaries. For the purpose of this analysis, however, these philosophical/psychological objections, like the scientific ones noted above, may be set aside in order to focus attention on the more properly theological aspects of Hodge's critique.

Of the theological issues commonly involved in the twentieth-century creation/evolution controversies, none is more peripheral for Hodge than the notion that the chronology of Genesis is to be taken literally. Although Hodge remains skeptical of geologists' claims about the age of the earth or the antiquity of humankind, by 1872 he has no theological objections to a geological time scale embracing "countless ages." Before his critique of Darwinism appeared in Volume II of *Systematic Theology*, he had already advocated in Volume I an interpretation of the Genesis "day" as "an indefinite period of time" to harmonize the biblical narrative with scientific evidence. Therefore, biblical chronology plays essentially no part in Hodge's critique of Darwinism.[36]

Equally peripheral for Hodge's critique (though for a different reason) is monogenism, the doctrine that all human beings are descended from one original progenitor. According to Hodge, monogenism is taught by the Bible and required by the doctrine of the fall. In the nineteenth century, however, the principal threat to monogenism was not Darwinism but polygenism, the theory that the human races constitute distinct species with separate origins. Agassiz, not Darwin, was the most prestigious advocate of polygenism. In fact, from Hodge's perspective Darwin was as far from being a polygenist as anyone could possibly be, going to the opposite (and equally false) extreme of advocating a common origin for humans and other animals. Therefore, Hodge does not object to Darwinism

as a denial of monogenism, and this issue is not
included in his critique.[37]

Only slightly less peripheral is another
theological issue involved in Hodge's view of the fall:
original perfection. For Hodge, the original
perfection of Adam implies two things which are
relevant here: on the one hand, Hodge believes that
Adam was created fully mature; and on the other hand,
Hodge believes that the fall was preceded by a golden
age rather than a primitive state of barbarism. In his
theological anthropology in *Systematic Theology*,
Hodge's remarks on these points suggest that he was
aware of the potential conflict between them and
Darwin's theory. Yet neither point becomes an explicit
reason for his rejection of Darwinism, perhaps because
even on his own terms both of them might be negotiable.
First, Genesis does not claim that Adam was created
physically mature, and the idea that he grew from
infancy was advocated by some early Christian
theologians. Second, even on scriptural terms, the
state of paradise before the fall could have been
called "barbarism" in the external sense that it was a
state of nature rather than of civilization; only
internal moral barbarism appears to be ruled out. In
any case, original perfection does not play a
significant role in Hodge's critique. In fact, none of
the biblical issues commonly associated with a
fundamentalist reading of Genesis plays a significant
role: chronology, monogenism, original perfection, and
the historical fall have virtually nothing to do with
Hodge's central objections to Darwinism. Clearly,
those who attribute Hodge's anti-Darwinian stand to
biblical fundamentalism are mistaken. Much more

significant in Hodge's critique, though still not most
central, is the immutability of species as a
<u>theological</u> claim. To the extent that Hodge regards
immutability as a conclusion reached by naturalists on
the basis of evidence, it functions as a scientific
objection to Darwinism; and to the extent that he
regards species as immutable by definition, it
functions as a philosophical objection; but to the
extent that Genesis teaches that certain forms of life
were directly created and not derived from other forms,
the immutability of species functions as a theological
objection, not only to Darwinism but also to evolution
in general. Hodge's theological claim for the
immutability of species, however, was a qualified one.
In *Systematic Theology* he asserts that only some
species ("natural" ones) were originally created,
leaving open the possibility that others might have
arisen from evolution; and in *What Is Darwinism?* he
goes even further, distinguishing "species" from
"primordial forms" and claiming original, underived
creation only for the latter. On this particular point
(though <u>not</u> on the issue of design), it is quite
conceivable that Hodge's quarrel with Darwin might
eventually have resolved itself into a dispute over the
number and character of primordial forms, rather than
an objection to evolution itself. In any case, the
immutability of species is clearly not the central
issue in Hodge's critique.

Another indication that the origin of at least some
species through evolution was not a central problem for
Hodge is that, as his position matured, he gradually
sharpened the distinction between Darwinism and
evolution and directed his criticisms more and more

specifically at the former. In his first published reference to Darwinism in 1862, Hodge made no distinction at all between that theory and evolution in general. Ten years later, in *Systematic Theology*, he distinguished the two but still occasionally confused them, as when he cited Argyll's evolutionism as an example of "a theistic interpretation of the Darwinian theory."[38] By 1874, however, the distinction is prominently featured on the very first page of *What Is Darwinism?*, and Hodge consistently distinguishes the two thereafter. Evidence that Hodge focused his attention more and more on Darwin's particular theory comes from a quantitative comparison of his critiques in *Systematic Theology* and *What Is Darwinism?*: the former devotes about as many pages to criticizing Darwin's theory as it does to criticizing evolution in general (a proportion of one to one), while in the latter the proportion shifts dramatically to about four to one. If sheer volume is any indication of emphasis, in comparison with Darwinism Hodge de-emphasized his criticism of evolution as his position matured.

Since it appears that Hodge's theological position on the immutability of species was flexible enough to accommodate some notion of evolution, especially if all that notion meant was (as McCosh had put it in 1873) "an exhibition of order running through successive ages," it is quite conceivable that he might eventually have adopted some form of theistic evolutionism, as did several of his successors at Princeton Seminary. This is speculation, however, and the fact remains that Hodge never accepted the general notion of evolution. Even as late as 1874, he suspected that no theory of evolution could be reconciled with the Bible. What was

it about evolution per se that Hodge found
unscriptural?

In *What Is Darwinism?*, Hodge quotes from Dawson
(who, like Hodge, had criticized Darwinism at the 1873
Evangelical Alliance Conference) to the effect that
"halfway evolutionism" which professes to be guided by
God is philosophically untenable. Dawson relied on
"the bare, hard logic of Spencer" to argue that there
is no room for compromise between a true doctrine of
creation and an evolutionism which attributes all
development to "unconscious" natural forces.
Apparently, Hodge likewise suspects that any consistent
theory of evolution, even one that admits an original
creation by God, would have to ascribe the origin of
species entirely to "blind, unintelligent physical
causes." In other words, a consistent theory would
presumably purport to explain the entire course of
evolution naturalistically. Hodge is obviously not
referring to the methodological principle that natural
science should restrict itself to the study of
observable causes, but to the substantive claim that
once it begins the evolutionary process is entirely
explicable (at least in principle) in naturalistic
terms. This, on Hodge's terms, should properly be
called deism, or "theism in unscriptural form."[39]

There are for Hodge, at least two theological
issues wrapped up in this objection. One is the origin
of the human soul. Hodge was a strict creationist in
this regard. Although in *Systematic Theology* he
maintains that the human body was "formed by the
immediate intervention of God," in *What Is Darwinism?*
he acknowledges the body as "a part of the universe"
and thus, conceivably, produced by the operation of

natural causes directed by God. The soul, however, is a spirit, "of the same nature with God," and thus "God-like." No physical causes could intervene in its creation, and thus no naturalistic theory of evolution which presumes to account for the spiritual nature of human beings would ever be acceptable to Hodge. That this is a central issue for him is evident from the fact that, systematically speaking, his theological attacks on "development" and evolution are located in his discussions of human origins.

By 1874, however, a second issue occupies considerably more of his attention: the conflict between naturalistic evolution and God's providential government. Although Hodge acknowledges that God's providential government is ordinarily exercised through the mediation of secondary physical causes, he insists on maintaining God's sovereign freedom to act without them. Hodge would thus look with extreme distrust on any theory (such as deistic evolution) which tends to leave no room, in principle, for God's unmediated intervention. Even more central, however, is Hodge's insistence that secondary causes cannot, by themselves, produce anything requiring intelligent design. The origin of significantly new forms of life, in Hodge's view, certainly requires intelligent design. Therefore, "blind, unintelligent physical causes" operating without God's guidance could not possibly produce them. To claim that they do amounts to a denial of God's providence. Since Hodge considers God's providential government to be one of the "principle fundamental doctrines of religion," second in importance only to the "being and perfections of God," such a claim would encounter a fundamental

theological objection.[40] Clearly, to the extent that
Hodge believes that any philosophically consistent
theory of evolution would have to make such a claim, he
must object to evolution in general.

Whether or not all theories of evolution deny God's
providential government, however, Hodge has no doubt
that Darwin's theory does so. One of the more central
theological issues in Hodge's critique, therefore, is
Darwin's implicit claim that "blind, unintelligent
physical causes" suffice to account for the origin of
species. This is not yet, however, the most central
issue for Hodge. Deistic theories of evolution which
attribute evolution to natural causes may still be
compatible with some notion of God's design. For
example, some naturalistic theories (such as Newtonian
mechanics) involve processes which can produce specific
preordained results. Although the "blind,
unintelligent physical causes" presumed to operate in
deistic evolution might be called "a-teleological," in
the sense that they can be studied and described
without any reference to purpose, they may at least be
of such a nature that their outcome may be designed.
In other words, deistic theories (though unscriptural)
could still be compatible with theistic notions about
the teleology of the evolutionary process as a whole.
Darwinism, however, according to Hodge, excludes even
this sort of teleology. Not only does Darwin's theory
attribute the evolutionary process to "blind,
unintelligent physical causes," but it also attributes
it primarily to a cause which is inherently anti-
teleological. Darwin's unique innovation is neither
evolution in general, nor even natural selection as one
cause among several, but the use of natural selection

in such a way as to rule out teleology completely. Hodge clearly considers this exclusion of design the "grand and fatal objection to Darwinism," and it provides the key to his central theological objection to the theory.

By "design," Hodge means the intelligent and voluntary selection of an end, and the intelligent and voluntary choice and control of means appropriate to achieve that end. He believes that the origin of any significantly new form of life involves design, both in the sense that it serves a definite end (the fulfillment of God's original plan, culminating in the creation of human beings in God's image), and in the sense that it is an act of creation utterly beyond the capability of "blind, unintelligent physical causes." Unfortunately, Hodge confuses matters by also listing biological reproduction as an example of a process involving design. He does so because he believes there is no "chemical substance" which could serve as the transmitter of heredity, and thus that God's purposeful agency must be involved in every individual case of propagation.[41] The twentieth-century discovery of DNA, of course, seems to solve this particular problem. It does not, however, significantly weaken Hodge's case: there is an obvious difference between reproduction (in which no new species is produced) and the origin of a new species. Even on Hodge's own terms, the former (except for the origin of the human soul) could be ascribed to the operation of "blind, unintelligent physical causes" without denying providence or design; the latter, however, in which not only a new individual but a new form of life arises, would require God's creative activity. Hodge would still maintain that reproduction is designed in the senses that (1) God designed the species as a whole, and (2) God designed the mechanism of reproduction for the purpose of propagating the species; but a theory of biological reproduction which does not deny design in these senses would not necessarily present a theological problem for Hodge, so long as the theory does not presume to account for the emergence of significantly new forms of life. And even if the theory did presume to do so, Hodge would have objected to it only as "theism in unscriptural form" because of its denial of providence. His objection to Darwin's theory is much more serious.

As Hodge understands it, Darwin's theory denies design as well as providence. Not only does Darwinism presume to account for the origin of species by the operation of "blind, unintelligent physical causes" (a denial of providence), but the particular causes invoked by Darwinism are also anti-telelological in the sense that they exclude the possibility that new species are designed by God. Naturalistic theories of evolution which exclude God's control or intervention, but which posit a mechanism that God could preordain to produce designed results, merely deny God's providential control of secondary causes; but according to Hodge, Darwin's theory posits a mechanism that is not only naturalistic, but also incapable of producing designed results. It thereby denies God's very existence.

Why would a denial of design be tantamount to a denial of God's existence? At first glance, the source of the problem might seem to be the teleological argument for the existence of God, the argument from design. Indeed, one passage in Volume II of *Systematic*

Theology seems to indicate that this is where Hodge locates it: he calls Darwinism atheistic on the grounds that there is "no more effectual way of getting rid of a truth than by rejecting the proofs on which it rests."[42] But this is the only passage in which Hodge makes such a statement, and it is a rather odd one for him to make, for several reasons. First, Hodge bases his knowledge of God far more on scriptural revelation and common-sense intuition than he does on rational proofs. Second, although he discusses the teleological argument at length in Volume I of *Systematic Theology*, his discussion never mentions Darwinism as a problem; and except for the implied reference in the passage cited above, his critique of Darwinism (in Volume II of *Systematic Theology*, in his remarks at the Evangelical Alliance Conference, and in *What Is Darwinism?*) never mentions the argument from design.

Third, if Hodge were to rely on the argument from design to prove that an exclusion of design amounts to a denial of God's existence, he would be guilty of an elementary mistake in logic. Although this is certainly a possibility, Hodge was not stupid, nor was he ignorant of elementary logic, and it seems unlikely that he would base his "grand and fatal objection to Darwinism" on such a mistake. The nature of the mistake becomes clear if the argument from design is summarized in the following form:

The Argument From Design

> If living organisms are designed, then
> God exists.
>
> Living organisms are designed.
>
> Therefore, God exists.

Hume and Kant had objected to the argument on the grounds that the first premise is invalid: although design in living organisms might prove the existence of a designer, it would not prove the existence of God. As Hodge interprets Darwin's theory, it would deny the second premise by claiming that living organisms are undesigned. According to elementary logic, however, a denial of either premise is not tantamount to a denial of God's existence: it merely denies that God's existence is proved by this particular argument. It might still be possible to establish God's existence on other grounds, or be consistent to believe in it on no grounds at all, even if the argument from design fails completely. Therefore, although the argument from design may be inadequate as a proof of God's existence, it cannot logically be grounds for denying that God exists.

Hodge's belief in God's existence, however, does not depend on the argument from design, nor does his belief that living organisms are designed depend on the findings of biological science. Although he cites some such findings in Volume I, and although he believes that design is there for all to see, his more fundamental claim is that it follows from scripture and the nature of God. The teachings of the Bible, and God's very being as the omnipotent, intelligent, and benevolent creator, imply design in living things. Since Hodge raises this point as in the context of his discussion of human origins, it is clear that he regards human beings, most of all, as designed by God.

In other words, design for Hodge is a theological conclusion rather than an empirically established premise. Although Hodge does not formulate it explicitly, what he is actually employing is an argument to design:[43]

The Argument To Design

If God exists, then living organisms are designed.

God exists.

Therefore, living organisms are designed.

The first premise in the argument from design is obviously different from its converse in the argument to design. The former extrapolates from the notion of designer to the God of Christianity, while the latter finds the notion of designer included in the Christian doctrine of God. The arguments differ even more in the second premise: one relies on purportedly empirical observations of design, while the other asserts God's existence on unspecified and independent grounds. The logical form of the two arguments, however, is similar.

Both are examples of the <u>modus</u> <u>ponens</u> of classical logic: in a hypothetical proposition (i.e., "if A then B"), affirming the antecedent ("A") necessarily entails affirming the consequent ("B").

How, then, does Darwin's theory deny the existence of God? Again, although Hodge does not formulate it explicitly, he is using an argument to design, but this time in its <u>modus</u> <u>tollens</u> form. In this form, denying the consequent necessarily entails denying the antecedent:

The Argument To Design
(Modus Tollens Form)

If God exists, then living organisms are designed.

(According to Darwinism), living organisms are not designed.

Therefore, (according to Darwinism) God does not exist.

According to classical logic, the conclusion necessarily follows from the premises: if God's existence entails design, and Darwinism denies design, Darwinism denies God's existence. It is true that Hodge did not present the argument in this explicit form, but the whole logic of his position assumes it implicitly. No theological issue, of course, could be as central for Hodge as the very existence of God; the existence of an omnipotent, intelligent, benevolent creator entails design in living organisms in general, and design of the human species in particular; by excluding design from the origin of species, Darwin's theory thus denies the very existence of God. This, then, is Hodge's "grand and fatal objection to Darwinism."

The mere fact that the argument is logically valid (i.e., that its conclusion follows from the premises), however, does not guarantee that it is sound. It is possible, for example, that Hodge's first premise was unique to his peculiar brand of nineteenth-century American Calvinism, and that for the majority of Christians God's existence does not entail the design Hodge claims. It is also possible that Hodge misunderstood Darwin's theory, or at least inferred unwarranted consequences from it. In either case, Hodge's conclusion might have little but historical interest for other Christians. On the other hand, if Hodge's premises are representative of "mainstream" Christianity and faithful to "orthodox" Darwinism (assuming that those rather vague entities can be adequately defined), then his conclusion might point to a basic conflict between Christian theology and Darwin's theory. Therefore, it would be of considerable interest to examine his premises more closely in an attempt to ascertain their adequacy.

NOTES

1.   Charles Hodge, *Systematic Theology* , 2:3-12.

2.   Hodge, *Systematic Theology*, 2:12-13.

3.   Hodge, *Systematic Theology*, 2:13-14. Hodge used the 1869 (fifth) London edition of Darwin's *Origin of Species*.

4.   Hodge, *Systematic Theology*, 2:14-15.

5.   Hodge, *Systematic Theology*, 2:15.

6.   Hodge, *Systematic Theology*, 2:15-19.

7.   Hodge, *Systematic Theology*, 2:19-22.

8.   Hodge, *Systematic Theology*, 2:22-26.

9.   Hodge, *Systematic Theology*, 2:26.

10. Hodge, *Systematic Theology*, 2:27-33.

11. Hodge, *Systematic Theology*, 2:30.

12. Hodge, *Systematic Theology*, 2:33-41.

13. Hodge, *Systematic Theology*, 2:77-93.

14. Schaff and Prime, eds., *History of the Evangelical Alliance*, iii.

15. Schaff and Prime, eds., *History of the Evangelical Alliance*, 264-271.

16. Schaff and Prime, eds., *History of the Evangelical Alliance*, 317-318.

17. "American Lights of the Evangelical Alliance," in *The Sunday School Times*, October 18, 1873. Excerpts published with permission of Princeton University Library.

18. Schaff and Prime, eds., *History of the Evangelical Alliance*, 318. The report undoubtedly should have read "unintelligent" rather than "unintelligible".

19. Schaff and Prime, eds., *History of the Evangelical Alliance*, 318.

20. Schaff and Prime, eds., *History of the Evangelical Alliance*, 272-287, 319-320.

21. Schaff and Prime, eds., *History of the Evangelical Alliance*, 320. The report undoubtedly should have read "undesigning" rather than "undesignating".

22. Schaff and Prime, eds., *History of the Evangelical Alliance*, 320-323.

23. Charles Hodge, *What Is Darwinism?*, 1-2.

24. Hodge, *What Is Darwinism?*, 3-7.

25. Hodge, *What Is Darwinism?*, 7-25.

26. Hodge, *What Is Darwinism?*, 26-27.

27. Hodge, *What Is Darwinism?*, 28-40. Hodge used the 1871 New York edition of Darwin's *Descent of Man*.

28. Hodge, *What Is Darwinism?*, 40-53.

29. Hodge, *What Is Darwinism?*, 53-125. Hodge used the 1868 New York edition of Darwin's Variation of Animals and Plants Under Domestication.

30. Hodge, *What Is Darwinism?*, 125-140.

31. Hodge, *What Is Darwinism?*, 141-151.

32. Hodge, *What Is Darwinism?*, 151-171.

33. Hodge, *What Is Darwinism?*, 169-177. See also Darwin, Variation of Animals and Plants Under Domestication, 2:515-516.

34. Charles Hodge, "Polemic Theology," 3-4, 9-10; Hodge, *Systematic Theology*, 2:12-13, 15-19; Hodge, *What Is Darwinism?*, 48, 177.

35. Hodge, *Systematic Theology*, 2:13-14; Hodge, *What Is Darwinism?*, 28-30; Darwin, *Origin Of Species*, 579.

36.   Hodge, *Systematic Theology*, 1:570-574, 2:33-41.

37.   Hodge, "Diversity of Species in the Human Race," 461;   Greene, *Death Of Adam* 221-247, 316-319, 327; Bowler, *Evolution: History of an Idea*, 282, 290-299.

38.   Hodge, "Diversity of Species in the Human Race," 461;   Hodge, *Systematic Theology*, 2:16.

39.   Hodge, *What Is Darwinism?*, 22, 119-123.

40.   Hodge, "Polemic Theology," 8.

41.   Hodge, *Systematic Theology*, 2:613;   Hodge, *What Is Darwinism?*, 171;   Hodge, "The First and Second Adam," 352-353.

42.   Hodge, *Systematic Theology*, 2:16.

43.   Some recent scholars maintain that even the argument from design is really an argument to design in disguise: belief in God induces the believer to see design in nature, which functions more as an expression of piety than as evidence for the original belief (see, for example, Dupre, A Dubious Heritage, 162-163).

CHAPTER FOUR
The First Premise: Christianity and the Argument to Design

The first premise of Hodge's critique of Darwinism is that God's existence entails design in living organisms. Is this claim valid only for Hodge's own peculiar brand of American Calvinism, or is it representative of "mainstream" Christianity as a whole? In order to answer this question, it is not necessary to determine whether God actually exists (a determination which, to say the least, would be beyond the scope of this essay), but only whether Christian belief in God entails the claim that living organisms are designed. It is important to note that this is a question about Christian belief, not about God or the world. In other words, for the purpose of the following analysis the issue is not whether God actually exists or whether living organisms actually are designed, but only whether design in living organisms is a consequence of Christian belief in God. As used here, "consequence" does not mean that the existence of living organisms is a consequence of God's existence, as though God had to create by necessity; it refers only to the claim that if God chooses to create living organisms, it follows from the Christian notion of God that those organisms are designed.

The word "design" can, of course, have several different meanings. It can refer to (1) the idea or pattern or plan, either in the mind of the designer or apart from it, according to which something is made; (2) the mental activity of the designer in formulating this idea or pattern or plan; (3) the deliberate or intentional activity by which the designer makes a thing; or (4) those aspects of the thing made which are the result of planned or intentional activity. Although Hodge would have recognized all four of these meanings, he explicitly defined design in terms of a pre-existent plan (1) and deliberate activity (3).

In addition to distinguishing these four different meanings of "design", it is also helpful to note some further distinctions in (4), since there are several different aspects of things which could be attributed to planned or intentional activity. For example, it is possible to say that one or more of the following are designed by God: (4a) the tendency of natural bodies to act for ends, to which Aquinas refers in his Fifth Way in the *Summa Theologiae*; (4b) the general order of the universe, to which Aquinas refers in his *Summa Contra Gentiles*; (4c) the distinctive characteristics of the major kinds of living things, such as the kinds enumerated in Genesis; (4d) each species of animal or plant; or (4e) every detail of every living thing, right down to the number of hairs on a head.[1]

One final distinction to be made here concerns the doctrine of providence. The notion of evolution tends to shift the origin of living things from the doctrine of creation to the doctrine of providence, both by extending it over time and by attributing it to the operation of secondary causes. Providence is thus relevant to the discussion in so far as it deals with God's control of secondary causes to produce designed results. The only result of interest here, however, is the origin of living organisms; providence as it applies specifically to events in human history can thus be ignored.

Although these distinctions do not, of course, constitute a rigorous analysis of the concept of design, they may help to prevent a certain amount of confusion in attempting to evaluate Hodge's first premise. Keeping them in mind, the question to be addressed here is: In what senses is design in living organisms a consequence of Christian belief in God's existence?

Any attempt to answer this question immediately encounters the difficulty of defining "Christian belief." Given almost any Christian doctrine, one could probably find some people who sincerely consider themselves to be Christian and yet take exception to that particular doctrine. Therefore, it may not even be possible to define "Christian belief" in terms which would be acceptable to all people who call (or have called) themselves "Christian."

This does not mean, however, that "Christian belief" must be regarded as completely amorphous. Certain basic doctrines, for example, are shared by the "mainstream" theological traditions of all three major branches of Christianity: Eastern Orthodoxy, Roman Catholicism, and Protestantism. The question to be addressed here is whether those shared doctrines entail the claim that God designed living organisms. One way to approach this question would be to examine the Bible and the early ecumenical creeds, which all three traditions consider normative, though in varying degrees, for doctrinal claims. A second way to

approach the question would be to survey the thought of
some theologians who could be considered broadly
representative of each tradition. A third way would be
to examine common criticisms of Hodge's own theology,
to ascertain whether they weaken or invalidate his
implicit claim to be representing Christianity as a
whole in this matter.

(1) The Bible and the Creeds

Appealing to the Bible to justify doctrinal claims
is, of course, fraught with difficulties. Christian
theologians differ greatly not only in their
interpretations of specific passages, but also in their
overall approaches to scripture. Even if the Bible
explicitly stated that God designed living things,
there could still be disagreement over what that claim
means, whether it is doctrinally authoritative, how it
should function in theological discourse, and so on.[2]
On the other hand, biblical passages which touch on
God's design of living organisms can hardly be ignored
here, especially since, for Hodge, "Christian" meant
"biblical." What follows, then, is a summary of some
relevant passages from the Bible and the early
ecumenical creeds, accompanied by a minimum of
interpretation. These scriptural and creedal passages
are among the ones Hodge uses in his *Systematic
Theology*, and they are probably among the "facts" he
would have used had he chosen to defend his implicit
claim that God's existence entails design in living
organisms.

Each of the two creation narratives in Genesis
begins with the initial creation of "the heavens and
the earth." In the first narrative (Genesis 1:1-2:3),

every subsequent creative act of God begins with the formula, "And God said: Let...," after which the specified creature begins to exist. Among the beings specifically created according to this formula are: light, the firmament, dry land, vegetation (including various "kinds" of plants and trees), the sun and moon, living creatures that move (including various "kinds" of aquatic animals, birds, and land animals), and, finally, human beings, which God makes "in our image, according to our likeness." In the second creation narrative (Genesis 2:4-2:25), God first "formed man of the dust of the ground," and thereafter caused to grow "every tree that is pleasant to the sight and good for food." In order that man should not be alone, God then "formed every beast of the field and every bird of the air," and finally made woman.[3]

In addition to Genesis, the books of Nehemiah, Psalms, and Isaiah contain important references to God's creatorship. For example, according to Nehemiah 9:6, "Ezra said: 'Thou art the Lord, thou alone; thou hast made heaven, the heaven of heavens, with all their host, the earth and all that is on it, the seas and all that is in them; and thou preservest all of them.'"

Numerous passages in the Psalms proclaim God the creator of all things: "By the word of the Lord the heavens were made, and all their hosts by the breath of his mouth" (Psalm 33:6). "O Lord, how manifold are thy works! In wisdom hast thou made them all; the earth is full of thy creatures" (Psalm 104:24). The Lord "made us, and not we ourselves; we are his people and the sheep of his pasture" (Psalm 100:3). More specifically, God "planted the ear" and "formed the eye" (Psalm 94:9). According to the psalmist, God even formed "my inward parts," and "knit me together in my mother's womb" (Psalm 139:13). Furthermore, God causes "the grass to grow for the cattle, and plants for man to cultivate, that he may bring forth food from the earth" (Psalm 104:14).

Similar themes are found in Isaiah: "The Lord is the everlasting God, the Creator of the ends of the earth" (Isaiah 40:28). It is God "who created the heavens and stretched them out, who spread forth the earth and what comes from it, who gives breath to the people upon it and spirit to those who walk in it" (Isaiah 42:5). It is "the Lord, your Redeemer, who formed you from the womb" (Isaiah 44:24). "Woe to him who strives with his Maker, an earthen vessel with the potter!" (Isaiah 45:9). "Thus says the Lord, the Holy One of Israel, and his Maker: 'Will you question me about my children, or command me concerning the work of my hands? I made the earth, and created man upon it'" (Isaiah 45:11-12).

In the New Testament, the prologue to the Gospel of John equates God the creator with God the incarnate Word: "In the beginning was the Word, and the Word was with God, and the Word was God. He was in the beginning with God; all things were made through him, and without him was not anything made that was made" (John 1:1-3). This theme is echoed by Colossians 1:15-16: "He is the image of the invisible God, the first-born of all creation; for in him all things were created, in heaven and on earth;" and it is also echoed by Hebrews 11:3: "By faith we understand that the world was created by the word of God, so that what is seen was made out of things which do not appear."

God "made the world and everything in it, being Lord of heaven and earth" (Acts 17:24). According to Paul, "ever since the creation of the world his invisible nature, namely, his eternal power and deity, has been clearly perceived in the things that have been made" (Romans 1:20).

In a discussion of the difference between physical and spiritual bodies, I Corinthians 15:38-39 distinguishes between the "kinds" of living things which God created: "God gives it a body as he has chosen, and to each kind of seed its own body. For not all flesh is alike, but there is one kind for men, another for animals, another for birds, and another for fish." Referring more specifically to human beings, Ephesians describes us as God's "workmanship," chosen "before the foundation of the world" for salvation through Jesus Christ (Ephesians 1:4, 2:10).

A seminal passage for the doctrine of God's providence is Matthew 10:29-31, which quotes Jesus as asking: "Are not two sparrows sold for a penny? And not one of them will fall to the ground without your Father's will. But even the hairs of your head are numbered. Fear not, therefore: you are of more value than sparrows."

The early ecumenical creeds affirm God's creatorship and providential control, but do not explicitly address the issue of design. The creed of Nicea (325 A.D.) affirms a belief in "one God, the Father All Governing, creator of all things visible and invisible," and in Jesus Christ, "through whom all things came into being, both in heaven and in earth." The creed of Constantinople (381 A.D.) includes essentially the same affirmations.[4]

A straightforward reading of these scriptural and creedal passages shows, at the very least, that it was not unreasonable of Hodge to infer that scripture warrants the claim that God's existence entails design in living organisms. Given the various ways in which scripture can be used in theological discourse, however, not to mention the possible variations in the interpretation of particular passages, these references cannot, by themselves, settle the issue of whether Hodge's argument to design is typical of the larger Christian tradition or limited to his own brand of American Calvinism. For this reason, it is important to examine the thought of some representative Christian theologians.

(2) Representative Theologians

The theologians chosen to represent each of the three major Christian traditions should, of course, be those who are most prominent and influential, rather than those who happen to hold the doctrine in question. For example, among the early fathers whom Eastern Orthodoxy considers theologically authoritative, Gregory of Nazianzus explicitly taught that God created all things according to pre-existing "forms," and Basil dealt with design in the creation at some length in his homilies on Genesis; but Athanasius, one of their contemporaries, is called "the Father of Orthodoxy" by the Greek Church, and is probably more prominent and influential in the tradition as a whole. Next to Athanasius, the best representative of Eastern Orthodox theology would perhaps be Maximus the Confessor (called "the real Father of Byzantine theology" by a modern authority on Eastern Christian thought).[5] Taking

Athanasius and Maximus as representative of Eastern
Orthodoxy, Augustine and Aquinas would then be the two
most obvious choices to represent traditional Roman
Catholicism, and Luther and Calvin the most obvious
representatives of classical Protestantism.

Modern liberal Protestant theology, though perhaps
not as distinct or major a tradition as the other
three, has been especially influenced by one of Hodge's
contemporaries, Friedrich Schleiermacher. Even
Schleiermacher's arch-critic, Karl Barth, concedes that
he "has no rival" in the history of modern theology.[6]
Therefore, it seems appropriate to add him to the list
of prominent theologians.

These seven theologians, then, can be considered
broadly representative of "mainstream" Christian
belief, at least up to the nineteenth century. What
follows is not intended to be a complete treatment, nor
even a balanced summary, of the thought of these seven
men, but merely a search for the argument to design in
their theologies. Do they argue from God's nature or
existence to design in the creation? If so, is design a
merely peripheral element in their theologies, or do
they consider design in living organisms to be a
consequence of Christian belief in God?

(a) Athanasius and Maximus

Athanasius developed his fourth-century theology
primarily in defense of the Nicene Creed and in
opposition to Arius and his followers. The Arians had
attempted to preserve God's absolute transcendence by
arguing that the Logos, or Son of God, was a created
intermediary between God and the rest of the creation.
Athanasius, convinced that redemption from sin was the

central theological issue, focused his attention on the
incarnation: God becomes man so that fallen mankind can
be redeemed from sin and be deified. In order for this
redemption and deification to be possible, however, the
incarnate one must be God, the creator of heaven and
earth, and not a created intermediary. For Athanasius,
the full divinity of the Logos was thus the basic
starting point for all Christian theology.[7]

According to Athanasius, the full divinity of the
Logos entails several consequences. First, it means
that the generation of the Logos must not have been an
act of God's will, as though God could have chosen to
be without the Logos or as though there could have been
a time when the Logos did not exist. To be fully
divine, the Logos must have been generated not by will
but by nature: "A man by counsel builds a house, but by
nature he begets a son; and what is in building began
to come into being at will, and is external to the
maker; but the son is proper offspring of the father's
essence, and is not external to him. "Therefore, the
fundamental difference between the Logos and the
creation is that the former is eternally generated by
nature, from God's own substance; while the latter is
produced by an act of God's will, and has a beginning
in time.[8]

The creation, then, unlike the Logos, is the result
of divine counsel or deliberation. Athanasius
emphatically rejects the notion that "things have come
into being of themselves, and in chance fashion," or
that things have originated independently of purpose.
On the contrary, "counselling goes before things which
once were not, as in the case of all creatures," and
the Son "is Himself the Living Counsel of the Father,

by which all things have come to be." The Son,
however, like the Father, is "unalterable and
unchangeable;" so the divine counsel is eternal, and
God's will and purpose were with God "before the
world." Whatever exists is thus preceded by "its
pattern in God."[9]

Athanasius repeatedly emphasizes that all things
were created <u>directly</u> by God. The Arians, it seems,
argued that God had to employ a created mediator to
make the world because (1) ordinary creatures could not
withstand the untempered power of God, and (2) God is
too transcendent to be directly involved in the details
of creation. For Athanasius, these claims denied the
very goodness and power of God. The first claim, he
argues, though true to some extent, ignores God's love
for creatures: "For they could not have endured His
nature, which was untempered splendour, even that of
the Father, unless condescending by the Father's love
for man He had supported them and taken hold of them
and brought them into existence." The second claim is
false, because if it were true it would tend to "prove
the weakness of the Maker, if He had not the power of
Himself to make the universe, but provided for Himself
an instrument from without." According to Athanasius,
God "is not wearied by commanding, nor is His strength
unequal to the making of all things." Furthermore, "it
is irreligious to suppose that He disdained, as if a
humble task, to form the creatures Himself which came
after the Son; for there is no pride" in God. Finally,
if God's providence extends to small details, so does
God's creative activity: "If then it be not unworthy of
God to exercise His Providence, even down to things so
small, a hair of the head, and a sparrow, and the grass

of the field, also it was not unworthy of Him to make
them. For what things are the subjects of His
Providence, of those He is Maker through His proper
Word."[10]

Since God's providence and creatorship extend "even
down to things so small," they extend a fortiori to the
human species. God not only "fashioned the race of
men" in "His own image," but also foresaw the fall and
provided for redemption: just as a wise architect would
make provisions for repairing a house "should it at any
time become dilapidated," so "in the same way prior to
us is the repair of our salvation founded in Christ."
In other words, the incarnation of the Logos in a human
body was predestined from eternity. Christ's body,
which "is of no different sort from ours," was thus
made, at the proper time, according to God's eternal
plan.[11]

Athanasius also makes other statements which could
be considered relevant to a general notion of
evolution. For example, he believes that the creation
was made in six days.[12] But this belief is more of an
isolated obiter dictum than a central theological
claim. By contrast, Athanasius' conclusions about
design in the creation follow necessarily from the
divinity of the Logos, the central doctrine in his
theology. The fundamental distinction between the
divine Logos and a created being is that the former is
generated from God's nature, while the latter
originates in an act of God's purposeful will.
Furthermore, God's providential control over even the
smallest details of creation is predicated upon the
fact that those details were purposefully created by
God. Finally, God's eternal purpose is most evident in

the creation of human beings in the divine image, and in the predestined incarnation of the Logos in human body.

Just as Athanasius wrote largely in opposition to Arianism, so Maximus the Confessor wrote largely in opposition to Origenism. In the third century, Origen had taught that since God must have been omnipotent from eternity, and could only be omnipotent in relation to creatures, God could never have been without the rational essences or souls of created beings. Furthermore, since God is one and unchangeable, the diversity and movement which now characterize the creation must have been caused not by God but by the free decisions of created beings. According to Origen, the corporeal universe originated when rational essences chose to resist God, and thereby fell away: souls whose sins were neither so serious as to become demons, nor so slight as to become angels, were then incarnated in a diversity of bodies ranging from "dumb animals" to "diviner natures," depending on how far they had fallen. The diversity in the world, then, is due entirely to "the diversity and variety in the movements and declensions of those who fell from that primeval unity and harmony in which they were at first created by God."[13]

A century after many of Origen's views were condemned at the Second Council of Constantinople (553), Maximus the Confessor provided Byzantine theology with an orthodox alternative to them. In opposition to Origen's implicit claim that God creates by necessity, Maximus relied on the Athanasian distinction between nature and will to reaffirm God's freedom. According to Maximus, the logoi, or patterns,

of all creatures exist eternally in the mind of God,
but they are the products of God's will rather than
God's nature. Maximus refers to the logoi as divine
"thoughts" or "wills;" and only the Logos, in which
they are united and harmonized, is eternally generated
by God's nature. At the appropriate time, God creates
substantial realities according to their pre-existent
logoi, which are thus the bases for diversity and
movement in the corporeal universe. Therefore, all
things are the intended products of God's creative act
rather than the unintended results of a fall. This
does not mean that every detail of every being conforms
perfectly to its pre-existent logos: Maximus allows for
some variation due to the tropos, or mode of existence,
which affects the extent to which a being actualizes
its eternal and unchanging logos. Nevertheless, by
affirming that God's will is the origin not only of all
created beings, but also of their pre-existent
patterns, Maximus safeguards God's sovereignty and
purposefulness.[14]

Human beings, in particular, are created according
to the will of God. Whereas Origen taught that human
bodies were the result of the fall of pre-existent
souls, Maximus holds that God creates body and soul
together. Though body and soul are distinguishable,
they are inseparable, and only together do they form a
complete species. The one constitutive factor for both
is the will of God, whose divinity is reflected in the
psychophysical unity of the whole human being, and not
just the soul.[15]

According to Maximus, the human being is designed
to be a microcosm in which the mental, spiritual, and
physical aspects of creation are united. Furthermore,

this microcosm is intended to unite with, and partake of, the divine nature, thereby uniting the world with its creator. This cosmic union, which is finally achieved in the incarnation of the Logos in Christ, is the fulfillment of God's original purpose for creating the universe. The incarnation was thus foreordained, independently of the fall, from eternity.[16]

For Maximus, then, design in the creation follows from God's freedom, sovereignty, and creatorship. This is not to say that creation is necessary: in opposition to Origenism, Maximus denies that created essences necessarily pre-exist eternally with God, and maintains that only the patterns of created beings pre-exist as eternal but freely willed thoughts in the mind of God. Furthermore, Maximus rejects Origen's view that the diversity of created beings is due to the fall, and affirms that God is the sovereign creator of that diversity, which is based on the pre-existent patterns in the divine mind. Therefore, although created beings in their various modes of existence may not perfectly conform to their eternal patterns, their basic forms are designed by God. The human body and soul are especially designed to be a microcosm in which all other aspects of creation find their unity with each other and with God; and the incarnation is the pre-ordained fulfillment of this unity.

(b) Augustine and Aquinas

Augustine developed his theology of creation largely in opposition to Manichaeism, just as Athanasius and Maximus had developed theirs in opposition to Arianism and Origenism, respectively. In the third century, Mani seems to have taught the eternal existence of two

distinct entities, light (good) and darkness (evil).
As a result of a conflict which arose between the two,
some elements of light were imprisoned in matter, which
belongs to the realm of darkness and evil. Human
beings, in particular, were created by the powers of
darkness to capture as much light as possible through
procreation, which is thus the instrument of evil.
Zoroaster, Buddha, Jesus, and Mani were sent to
liberate the elements of light from their corporeal
prisons. Eventually, the conflict will subside, and
the light and the darkness will again co-exist side by
side.[17]

After converting from Manichaeism to Christianity
in the fourth century, Augustine devoted much of his
effort to combatting this cosmogonic dualism.
According to Augustine, the creator of all that exists
is God: "Whatever is, since it is, and in whatever
degree it is, has its existence from the one God." In
defense of God's sovereignty, Augustine insists that
all created beings have their forms or rationes
aeternae in "the very mind of the Creator." All things
are thus made according to God's eternal and unchanging
plan: "Because therefore the Word of God is One, by
which all things were made, which is the unchangeable
truth, all things are simultaneously therein,
potentially and unchangeably; not only those things
which are now in this whole creation, but also those
which have been and those which shall be." In other
words, "the Wisdom of God, by which all things have
been made, contains everything according to design
before it is made."[18]

In opposition to the Manichaeans, Augustine
maintains that God's creatorship extends to all forms

of existence: "even the lowest form is of God. And the same may be said of species." The "lowliest and smallest creatures are obviously fashioned by such a remarkable plan that a moment's serious attention to them fills the beholder with inexpressible awe and wonder;" and if they appear to us to be tiny and contemptible, it may only be that "on account of our pride, God appointed that tiny and contemptible creature to torment us." But if God's design extends even to the lowest forms of life, it extends a fortiori to human beings, who were "certainly" created in the form which God foreordained "before the ages."[19]

It is not completely clear, however, whether Augustine believes that foreordination extends to the precise form of every individual. When asked if "the Son of God contains within Himself the form of man in general, or each of us in particular," Augustine replies that "if we consider the creation of man as such, there is in Him the form of man only, not yours or mine; but if we consider the sequence of time, there exists in that absolute perfection the various forms of men." Augustine admits that "this is far from clear," but it may correspond to the distinction he makes elsewhere between creation and God's administration, whereby natural processes are directed in such a way as to fulfill the overall divine plan, though perhaps in such a way that God does not determine every detail of every organism. Regardless of this ambiguity, however, it is clear that Augustine considers human beings and every other kind of creature to be designed by God: "all things are created on a rational plan, and man not by the same rational plan as horses, for it is absurd

to think this.   Therefore individual things are created
in accord with _rationes_ unique to them."[20]

According to Augustine, God's act of creating the
world was timeless and instantaneous, and the six days
of Genesis are interpreted as a progressive revelation
of something which actually took place all at once.
Since plants and animals, however, evidently appeared
later than the earth and heavenly bodies, God must have
created them "potentially, in their causes," so that
what was created in the first instant could appear
later, in the course of time.   Augustine calls these
causes _rationes seminales_.[21] According to some modern
commentators, this notion justifies calling Augustine
the "Father of Evolution," though others reject this
designation on the grounds that the transformation of
one species into another is totally alien to
Augustine's way of thinking.[22]

Fortunately, for the purpose of this analysis it is
not necessary to resolve this dispute.   To the extent
that Augustine's notion of the _rationes seminales_
reflects his conviction that God's designing activity
is deliberate or intentional, it is relevant here.   It
is not particularly relevant, however, whether
Augustine is considered a static creationist or a
proto-evolutionist: the issue is not whether God
created instantaneously or over time, nor even whether
the mode of God's activity is consistent with
naturalistic theories of evolution, but only whether
and in what senses God designed living organisms.

In any case, Augustine's notion of the _rationes
seminales_ is a comparatively minor element in his
theology.   By contrast, his notion of the _rationes
aeternae_ is central to his refutation of Manichaeism

and to his doctrine of God. God is the only creator, wise and omnipotent, by whose will all things are made according to an eternal and unchanging plan. This divine plan extends even to the lowest forms of life, and certainly includes human beings. There may be some uncertainty whether the divine plan extends to every detail of every individual being, but there can be no doubt, for Augustine, that it includes every kind of living thing.

Writing more than eight centuries after Augustine, Thomas Aquinas developed his theology at a time when Latin Christianity was being confronted by a significant increase in the availability of the works of Aristotle. To the extent that Christian theology before Aquinas had made use of Greek philosophy, it had relied predominantly on Neoplatonism, which with its emphasis on a transcendent realm of perfect and eternal "forms" or "ideas" seemed quite adaptable to the Christian doctrine of God. Augustine's notion of the rationes aeternae was just such an adaptation, though unlike Plato or the Neoplatonists, Augustine placed the ideas in the mind of the supreme deity.[23]

Aristotle, however, rejected the Platonic doctrine of ideas, or at least the version of that doctrine which he attributed to Plato. Since Aquinas endeavored to synthesize Christian theology with Aristotelianism rather than Neoplatonism, it might be expected that he would similarly reject the Augustinian doctrine of ideas. Quite to the contrary, however, Aquinas considers it "necessary to suppose ideas in the divine mind," just as "the likeness of a house pre-exists in the mind of the builder." According to Aquinas, things receive their determinate forms because "in the divine

wisdom are the types of all things, which types we have
called ideas, - i.e., exemplar forms existing in the
divine mind."[24]

Although Aquinas concedes that this "saves to some
extent the opinion of Plato and his doctrine of Ideas,"
he agrees with much of Aristotle's critique of the
Platonic doctrine. For example, like Aristotle,
Aquinas objects to the Platonic notion that forms can
be posited as existing in themselves, since "the forms
of natural things cannot exist without matter."
Furthermore, like Augustine, Aquinas objects both to
the Platonic notion that the forms have separate
existences, and to the Neoplatonic placement of them in
a subordinate divine mind. On the other hand, Aquinas
does not equate the divine ideas with Aristotelian
forms: since "matter is caused by God," it is
"necessary to affirm that its exemplar in some way
exists in God," or, more precisely, that the divine
mind contains an idea of the entire composite of form
and matter. Thus for Aquinas, as for Augustine, the
divine ideas correspond neither to Platonic forms nor
to Aristotelian forms: they are not Platonic because
they exist only in the mind of God, and they are not
Aristotelian because they are ideas of the material as
well as the formal aspects of things.[25]

The fact that Aquinas' view of the divine ideas
resembles Augustine's, however, does not mean that
Aquinas merely incorporated the doctrine in his
theology out of respect for authority. Although the
language may be borrowed from Augustine, the concept
follows directly from central aspects of Aquinas'
doctrine of God. First, it follows from God's
intelligent, purposeful, and free creatorship. Since

"the world was not made by chance, but by God acting by
His intellect," therefore "there must exist in the
divine mind a form to the likeness of which the world
was made. And in this the notion of idea consists."
The doctrine safeguards God's intelligent
purposefulness, since it necessarily implies previous
planning in the production of creatures, and "those who
say that all things happen by chance cannot admit the
existence of ideas." It also safeguards God's freedom,
in opposition to the notion that the world emanates by
necessity from God's nature. Creatures pre-exist in
God's nature only "after the mode of intellect," but
they "proceed from Him after the mode of will." Since
"a form considered by the intellect does not move or
cause anything except through the will," it is God's
free will and not God's nature which determines what is
actually created.[26]

Second, the doctrine of ideas is implied in the
doctrine of the trinity, since "in the Word is implied
the operative idea of what God makes." Just as there
"pre-exists in the mind of a craftsman a certain image
of his external work," so also does there "pre-exist in
the mind of one who pronounces an exterior word a
certain archetype of it." This archetype, or "interior
word," is the Word of God; and the ideas of things to
be made are thus metaphorically called the Word of God.
Aquinas interprets the prologue to the Gospel of John
accordingly: "In the beginning was the Word" means that
things originate from God's intellect and purpose, "and
not from chance." This implies the doctrine of divine
ideas, but "the Word was with God" excludes Plato's
notion that ideas have separate existences, while "the

Word was God" excludes the Neoplatonic notion that the ideas were in a mind subordinate to God the Father.[27]

Third, the doctrine of ideas solves the problem of how God, who is supremely one, can nevertheless know and create a multitude of distinct things. Aquinas clearly affirms not only that God is one, but also that "the divine intellect understands by no species other than the divine essence." In order for God's knowledge to be absolutely perfect, however, God must know "all things with proper knowledge, in their distinction from each other." This is possible because "the divine essence is the likeness of all things," so that by knowing the divine essence God can understand a multitude of things. Furthermore, "the knowledge of God, joined to His will, is the cause of things." Since the order of the universe is intentionally caused by God, the divine mind "must have the idea of the order of the universe." But an idea of a whole presupposes ideas of its parts, "just as a builder cannot conceive the idea of a house unless he has the idea of each of its parts." Therefore, it must be "that in the divine mind there are the proper ideas of all things." This plurality of ideas "is not repugnant to the simplicity of the divine mind," since in a sense there is only one all-encompassing idea; but this one idea contains, in "an intelligible mode," the distinctions between things, so that "many ideas exist in the divine mind, as things understood by it."[28]

So "the form of the universe is intended and willed by God," and "the form of the universe consists in the distinction and order of its parts." Does this mean that every detail of every creature is designed by God? For Aquinas, "the distinction of species is derived from the form, and the distinction of singulars of the same species is from matter." Species are certainly designed by God, since "the form of any thing proceeding from an intellectual and voluntary agent is intended by that agent." Aquinas grants, however, that some individual distinctions, which are due to matter, "can be the result of chance." Furthermore, it is questionable whether Aquinas would consider every biological species to be designed by God, since he uses "species" in a philosophical rather than a biological sense. One modern commentator goes so far as to argue that there are really only five species for Aquinas: human beings, animals, plants, mixtures, and elements. Even on this minimal reading, however, the human species, at least, would have its exemplar in God. Furthermore, Aquinas explicitly affirms that the human soul is "made to the image of God," and that "God fashioned the human body" in order to "make it suitably proportioned to the soul."[29]

Thus, despite his shift to an Aristotelian rather than a Neoplatonic philosophical base, Aquinas retains the Augustinian doctrine of divine ideas. Not only are ideas implied by the notion that God creates intelligently, purposefully, and freely, but they are also implied in the doctrine of the trinity. The divine ideas also represent Aquinas' solution to the problem of how the supremely one God could know and create a multitude of distinct things. Throughout these discussions of the doctrine of ideas, one element remains constant: for Aquinas, as for Augustine, the Christian notion of God entails the claim that created beings, in their distinctions from each other as well as in their general order, are designed by God.

128

Although chance may cause differences between
individuals, species are produced by design; and
although what Aquinas means by "species" is subject to
debate, there can be no doubt that he considers the
human species, at least, to be designed by God.

(c) Luther and Calvin

Luther conceived of his sixteenth-century theology
as a return to the Christian tradition, from which, in
his opinion, the Roman Catholic Church had deviated.
Its deviation consisted, according to Luther, in over-
emphasizing the authority of the Papacy and
magisterium, and in burdening Christians with the
impossible task of having to earn their salvation by
doing works of penance. Luther's corrective for the
first deviation was to insist on scripture alone as the
authority for faith and practice, and his corrective
for the second was to make justification by faith alone
the most prominent doctrine in his theology.[30]

According to Luther, the essential teaching of the
Old and New Testaments is that we are totally dependent
on God in Christ. Since we are totally dependent, and
can do nothing for ourselves, our only hope is to have
complete faith in God's power and benevolence; and
through this faith God justifies us despite our
sinfulness, and without the need for works of penance.
Even faith is not our own doing, but God's work in us
through the Word. The doctrine of justification by
faith alone thus presupposes our total dependence on
God; but this, in turn, presupposes that we owe our
very existence to God. In this sense, the most
prominent doctrine in Luther's theology is directly

related to the more fundamental belief that God alone is the creator.[31]

For God to be the creator means, for Luther, that "the creation is not fortuitous but the exclusive work of divine foresight." From all eternity, God "has a Word, a speech, a thought, or a conversation with Himself in His divine heart;" and from this conversation, "heaven and earth, all creatures, both the visible and the invisible, come into being." Therefore, "all His works are some words of God, created by the uncreated Word." Since God creates out of nothing, which means without the need for any instrumentality or pre-existing material, Luther considers creation to be "a kind of birth." This birth, however, takes place "at the command of God," as a product of God's will rather than as a pantheistic emanation from God's nature. But Luther is less concerned with issues such as this than he is with the immediate significance of the doctrine of creation for the faith of the believer: we should know, for example, that even "great sea animals" are created by God, "lest we be frightened;" then "we may more readily believe that God can preserve us too, even though we are far smaller beings." Similarly, according to Luther, God tells us in Isaiah 40:28, "I have made all these things, they are my creatures, they are under My control, they cannot touch the least hair of your head. Do not be afraid." God's creatorship, then, means that "we must take note of God's power that we may be completely without doubt about the things which God promises in His word."[32]

It is not merely the initial creation of the universe which demonstrates God's power. Luther explains that God is not like a carpenter who "turns over the house to its owner" when he finishes constructing it; instead, God "continues to preserve His creation through the Word." In fact, "if the Creator, who continues to work forever and ever, and His Co-worker were to interrupt Their work, all would go to wrack and ruin in a twinkling." Luther draws from this the lesson that "as we human beings did not create ourselves, so we can do nothing at all to keep ourselves alive for a single moment by our own power. The fact that I grow and develop is God's work alone," and Luther means this in the strongest possible sense. He even interprets Isaiah 44:24 as being equivalent to a statement by God that "whatever is done, I alone have done it."[33] Modern commentators point out that, for Luther, God is thus the only true agent. God does absolutely everything, and whatever happens is a direct result of God's activity. Therefore, created beings are what Luther calls larva dei, or visible masks of the invisible God, testifying to God's omnipresent power, and encouraging us to "fear and trust only in God."[34]

Fortunately, however, we can trust in God's benevolence as well as God's power, since "all things were created as an aid to the mind and heart of man." In fact, in the beginning "God created all these things in order to prepare a house, and an inn, as it were, for the future man." Seeing the world from this perspective leads us to "reflect on the divine solicitude and benevolence toward us, because He provided such an attractive dwelling place for the future human being before the human being was created." Such reflection, in turn, leads to the complete trust

in God which, for Luther, is the ultimate goal of
theology: "And this generosity is intended to make man
recognize the goodness of God and live in the fear of
God."[35]

Given Luther's belief that God does all and
creatures can do nothing, it is unlikely that he would
attribute even the smallest detail of creation to
anything other than God's purposeful activity. Among
the forms of life that he specifically attributes to
God's design are "herbs and trees," which were created
"for our sustenance." He also considers the mouse to
be "created by the Word of God with a definite plan in
view," so that "here, too, we admire God's creation and
workmanship." Furthermore, "the same thing can be said
about flies." Above all, however, man and woman were
"created by the special plan and providence of God,"
specifically "for the knowledge and worship of God."[36]

Faith in God the creator, to whose power all things
owe their existence and to whose benevolence we owe our
sustenance, is thus intimately connected to Luther's
doctrine of justification by faith alone. We can trust
in God completely for our salvation, because everything
that happens is the work of God, and because God has
designed everything in creation for our benefit. God's
design provides the grounds for our trust, not in the
sense that empirical evidence of design might prove the
existence of God, but in the sense that our attitude of
trust is predicated upon faith in God's design. For
Luther, then, faith in God entails the faith that
living organisms are designed by God.

Calvin, like Luther, considers scripture (as
interpreted with the aid of the Holy Spirit) the only
reliable source for knowledge of God, at least since

the fall. If the fall had not occurred, our knowledge of God could have come from the creation, since God "discloses himself in the whole workmanship of the universe," which is thus "a sort of mirror in which we can contemplate God, who is otherwise invisible." God's workmanship includes "living beings and inanimate things of every kind," and "he endowed each kind with its own nature, assigned functions, appointed places and stations." The resulting creation is a "theater of the divine glory," but because of the fall "we have not the eyes to see this unless they be illumined by the inner revelation of God through faith." Once we have been given the "spectacles" of scripture, however, "the most perfect way of seeking God" is "to contemplate him in his works." This is an argument to design: through the eyes of faith the believer sees design in the creation, which then nourishes that faith in return. Thus "although it is not the chief evidence for faith, yet it is the first evidence in the order of nature, to be mindful that wherever we cast our eyes, all things they meet are works of God, and at the same time to ponder with pious meditation to what end God created them."[37]

Of all God's works, the "most excellent example" is humankind. Calvin interprets the "let us make man" of Genesis 1:26 as God's way of "commending to our attention the dignity of our natures," since God made all other creatures by command, but "enters into consultation" before making us. Furthermore, human beings are created in the divine image, the "chief seat" of which is in the mind and heart, though some "scintillations" shine in every part, including the body. Human beings are especially created "to seek

God" and "to behold the works of God," and they are
endowed with reason and understanding "that they might
acknowledge their Creator." The rest of the universe,
in turn, was "established especially for the sake of
mankind." According to Calvin, "the world was
originally created for this end, that every part of it
should tend to the happiness of man." God "filled the
earth, waters, and air with living things, and brought
forth an abundance of fruits," and thereby "shows his
wonderful goodness toward us." God could have created
the world in an instant, but devoted six days to
creation in order to "commend his providence and
fatherly solicitude toward us in that, before he
fashioned man, he prepared everything he foresaw would
be useful and salutary for him."[38]

Calvin emphasizes that God not only created but
also preserves and governs the world. In fact,
according to Calvin, God completely controls all
events. Without denying the existence of secondary
causes, Calvin nevertheless insists that "nothing
happens except what is knowingly and willingly decreed"
by God. Calvin specifically objects not only to those
who would "substitute nature for God" by making nature
"the artificer of all things," but also to those who
would attribute anything less than absolute control to
God. Included in this latter category are people who
"in place of God's providence substitute bare
permission -- as if God sat in a watchtower awaiting
chance events," as well as people who attribute to God
a providence which merely "by a general motion revolves
and drives the system of the universe" but which "does
not specifically direct the action of individual
creatures." For Calvin, God "so regulates all things

that nothing takes place without his deliberation," and "not one drop of rain falls without God's sure command." Unlike Aquinas, Calvin thus excludes chance altogether. What may appear to be a chance occurrence is "only that of which the reason and cause are secret," and the secret cause is God's foreordination. Though "for us they are fortuitous," such events are "governed by God's incomprehensible plans." Calvin considers this total governance by God a source of comfort to the believer, since it brings "gratitude of mind for the favorable outcome of things" and "freedom from worry about the future."[39]

Like Luther, Calvin is primarily interested in the practical consequences of theology for the believer: the knowledge of God, whether from scripture or creation, "invites us first to fear God, then to trust him." The believer thereby learns to worship and obey God, and to "depend wholly upon his goodness." Calvin is much less interested in speculating about God's knowledge of creatures than, say, Augustine, and he criticizes the latter for being "excessively addicted" to the Platonic doctrine of ideas.[40] But this does not mean that design is any less prominent in Calvin's theology than in Augustine's. The fear and trust which Calvin seeks to instill in the believer depend on God's omnipotence and benevolence, which are thus the most prominent attributes of God in Calvin's theology, and design is a direct consequence of those attributes. Design is a consequence of omnipotence because everything is under God's control, and nothing happens except what God purposefully causes to happen. Design is also a consequence of benevolence, in the sense that God created the entire universe for our benefit, preparing everything necessary for our happiness before creating us. Furthermore, since there is no such thing as chance for Calvin, God presumably designed every detail of every living thing.

(d) Schleiermacher

Three centuries after the Reformers, Schleiermacher refashioned the doctrine of God in response to the philosophical challenges of the Enlightenment. He has been called "the Kant of Protestant theology," in the sense that he set out to trim the pretensions of metaphysics in theological thinking just as Kant had done in philosophical thinking. Furthermore, Kant's turn to the subject in philosophy had its counterpart in Schleiermacher's emphasis on religious self-consciousness in theology. Like Kant, Schleiermacher was convinced that religion is not based on an intellectual knowledge of God, though unlike Kant he did not base religion on a moral imperative.[41] According to Schleiermacher, the basis of religion is "neither a Knowing nor a Doing, but a modification of Feeling, or of immediate self-consciousness." More specifically, it is "the consciousness of being absolutely dependent, or, which is the same thing, of being in relation to God." Christianity in particular is distinguished from religion in general by its monotheism and its "predominating reference to the moral task," but especially by the fact that "in it everything is related to the redemption accomplished by Jesus of Nazareth."[42]

Schleiermacher's system of Christian dogmatics includes three categories of propositions: "descriptions of human states," "conceptions of divine attributes and modes of action," and "utterances regarding the constitution of the world." He considers the first category (statements about religious self-consciousness) to be "the fundamental dogmatic form," while the second and third categories (statements about God and the world) are "permissible only in so far as they can be developed out of propositions of the first form." Schleiermacher is convinced that the second and third categories could eventually "be dispensed with altogether," since "they do not express anything that is not in its essential content already contained in the basic propositional form." This does not mean, however, that the theologian can say nothing about God or the world: Schleiermacher maintains that the feeling of absolute dependence cannot exist apart from God's absolute causality, and that on the basis of that inseparable connection we can therefore make true statements about God. Furthermore, since "no Christian religious emotion can be imagined in experiencing which we do not find ourselves placed in a nature-system," statements about religious self-consciousness may also be statements about the world. Whatever is said dogmatically about God or the world, however, must be derived from religious experience, and in no way proceed "from the speculative activity." Schleiermacher utilizes this principle in the hope of purging Christian doctrine of the alien metaphysics and primitive mythology which have exposed it to philosophical and scientific attack.[43]

Applying this principle to the Christian doctrine of creation, Schleiermacher concludes that "the proposition, 'God has created,' considered in itself," belongs to dogmatics "only so far as creation is

complementary to the idea of preservation," since
creation implies absolute dependence "only for the
beginning, with the exclusion of development."
Although the concept of creation can serve a negative
function by excluding cosmogonic dualism and
pantheistic monism, it suggests an event in the remote
past which by its very nature cannot be part of
religious experience. As such, the concept leads to
mythology and speculation which contribute nothing to
Christian piety and tend to ensnare theology in
"useless controversies." Schleiermacher prefers
"handing over this subject to natural science, which,
carrying its researches backward into time, may lead us
back to the forces and masses that formed the world, or
even further still." This means that "we must learn to
do without what many are still accustomed to regard as
inseparably bound to the essence of Christianity,"
including "the concept of creation itself." The
doctrine of creation thus has little dogmatic value for
Schleiermacher, unless it is interpreted as continual
creation, in which case it can be "completely absorbed
in the doctrine of Preservation."[44]

In the doctrine of preservation, the religious
self-consciousness places "all that affects or
influences us in absolute dependence on God," but this
"coincides entirely with the view that all such things
are conditioned and determined by the interdependence
of nature." In other words, "divine preservation, as
the absolute dependence of all events and changes on
God, and natural causation, as the complete
determination of all events by the universal nexus, are
one and the same thing simply from different points of
view." Schleiermacher maintains that if we were to

138

distinguish between divine and natural causality in such a way as to make the latter understandable without the former, or to understand the former as overruling or intervening in the latter, then "as our knowledge of the world grew perfect, the development of the pious self-consciousness in ordinary life would cease," and this would "contradict the principle that the observation of creation leads to the consciousness of God."[45]

Since the religious self-consciousness cannot conceive of anything, not even God, as apart from the world, divine and natural causality are thus equivalent in compass. In other words, it is not the business of dogmatics to speculate about what God _can_ _do_ apart from what God actually _does_, and Schleiermacher maintains that the divine causality should thus be thought of as "completely presented in the totality of finite being," so that "everything for which there is a causality in God happens and becomes real." On the other hand, God's causality must not be reduced to natural causality. Since the religious self-consciousness does not equate God with the world (otherwise the world would not be absolutely dependent on God), divine and natural causality are "entirely different". According to Schleiermacher, the equivalence of the two is "expressed in the term, the divine omnipotence," while the non-equivalence of the two is "expressed in the term, the divine eternity." The divine eternity does not mean that God existed before the world, but that God is "utterly timeless". Similarly, God is not outside the world but is "completely spaceless." Therefore, God and the world are not identical, and

Schleiermacher vehemently rejects the charge that his theology is pantheistic.[46]

In God's eternal omnipotence, there is no distinction between means and ends. Means "are never employed except where the agent has to have recourse to something not originated by himself." According to Schleiermacher, a good way to avoid thinking of God's activity in terms of means and ends is to think of the world as "an absolutely harmonious divine work of art": if "every human work of art is the more perfect, the more it conforms to the idea that elements within it should not be distinguishable asends and means," then there should be no such distinction in God's activity.[47]

God's eternal omnipotence also excludes, for Schleiermacher, the notion that God is like an artificer who contemplates and plans before acting. God is omniscient, in the sense that "the divine causality should be thought of as absolutely living," and God acts freely, since "He on Whom everything is absolutely dependent is absolutely free;" but these must not be understood as implying "a prior deliberation followed by choice." Since "there is for Him no succession, it can never be said that in Him the purposive thought-activity precedes the will-activity." Therefore, "there can be in God no distinction between resolving and the execution of the resolve." Schleiermacher thus rejects the traditional doctrine of "the existence of forms in God prior to the existence of things," as well as the notion that God knows possibilities which are never actualized. He maintains that it would be better "to transfer to God, illimited and perfect, the certainty of the perfect artist, who

in a state of inspired discovery thinks of nothing
else, to whom nothing else offers itself, save what he
actually produces." Once again, it is better to think
of the world as a spontaneous work of divine art,
rather than a planned work of divine engineering.[48]

This does not mean, however, that God's activity
has no purpose or goal. Schleiermacher maintains that
"an omnipotence, the aim and motive force of which I do
not know," and "an omniscience, the structure and value
of its contents I do not know," are "merely vague and
barely living ideas." In other words, "belief in God
as almighty and eternal," without knowing God's motive,
would be merely a "shadow of faith," in contrast to the
Christian faith, for which God is, above all,
absolutely loving. Schleiermacher's system of
Christian dogmatics thus reaches its culmination in the
doctrines of divine love and divine wisdom. Love is
"the attribute in virtue of which the divine nature
imparts itself," and wisdom is "the principle which
orders and determines the world." In other words, love
is the motive of omnipotence, and wisdom is the content
of omniscience. Furthermore, "love and wisdom alone"
are "not mere attributes but also expressions of the
very essence of God." In the government of the world,
the divine love and wisdom are directed towards a
single goal, which is "the Church, or the Kingdom of
God," and Schleiermacher speaks in terms of
"predestination" and "fore-ordination" in this
regard.[49]

The divine government extends to all things, since
all things are created "with a view to the revelation
of God in the flesh" and to the establishment of the
Kingdom of God. Christian dogmatics, however, can

speak of the divine government only in relation to
redemption, and Schleiermacher warns us "to be on our
guard against ascribing to divine wisdom the divine
ordering of external and physical nature" in such a way
as to "separate them from the sphere of redemption."
In other words, "the divine ordering of the world"
should be interpreted only "by reference to the
revelation of God in Christ and the Holy Spirit," and
"this ought never to degenerate into an inquisitive
search (unfriendly to scientific inquiry) with a view
to discovering particular aids to the Kingdom of God in
particular events." On the other hand, we have not
"fathomed the divine wisdom" if we suppose that it
could ever "conflict with the highest interests of
man." Thus while Schleiermacher discourages
speculation about what aspects of the world might be
specifically ordered by the divine wisdom, he clearly
affirms that the incarnation and human welfare are the
goal of the divine government.[50]

In what sense, then, -- if any -- would
Schleiermacher be willing to grant that God's existence
entails design in living organisms? The very notion of
design is problematical, since he excludes any
distinction in God between thinking and acting; and
according to one modern commentator "it is by no means
clear that he believed there is a personal being able
to comprehend purposes and devise a plan to realize
them."[51] Despite Schleiermacher's cautious language,
however, most commentators maintain that he does
ascribe the equivalent of purpose or intention to God.
One recent writer even concludes that, since "Jesus
Christ appears here as an individual belonging to an
all-inclusive harmony, to an arrangement that exhibits

the divine wisdom," in practice "design is a more
operative 'attribute' in Schleiermacher's system of
Christian doctrine than is divine love construed as
redemptive love."[52]

Would Schleiermacher be willing to say that God's
purpose or intention extends to specific aspects of
living organisms? On the one hand, Schleiermacher warns
that Christian doctrine can consider the divine
causality and government only as related to redemption,
and cautions against claiming that particular details
in the natural order are specifically ordained by God.
On the other hand, the centrality of redemption does
require divine ordination of at least one detail: the
incarnation of God in Jesus of Nazareth. Furthermore,
it is impossible to imagine how the Church could be the
eternal goal of the divine government unless the human
species as a whole is ordained by God. Therefore,
although Schleiermacher would rule out speculation
about other living things, it seems that he would have
to grant that the Christian religious self-
consciousness considers the fundamental eternal
motivation of the divine causality to be the creation
and redemption of human beings.

This survey of the thought of seven prominent
representatives of the major Christian theological
traditions indicates that the argument to design is
found in all of them, though in various forms. For
Athanasius, design is a consequence of the distinction
between the divinity of the Logos and the
creatureliness of the universe: the former is eternally
generated from God's nature, while the latter is
produced in time according to God's deliberate will.

For Maximus, design follows from God's sovereign creatorship: all things are deliberately created according to patterns or thoughts in the mind of God, not as the accidental result of an Origenistic fall of pre-existent souls. For Augustine, design is a consequence of monotheism: in opposition to Manichaean dualism, he insists that God is the creator of all things, and that their forms pre-exist in the divine mind. For Aquinas, the divine ideas according to which God creates insure that the universe is not the product of chance; they are also implied by the doctrine of the trinity, and they explain how a multitude of distinct things can come from the unity of God. For Luther, the absolute trust in God which is the most prominent feature of his theology is predicated upon the faith that everything that happens is the work of God and that God designed the universe for our benefit. Similarly, for Calvin, God's omnipotence and benevolence mean that all events are controlled by God in accordance with the secret divine plan, and that all things were created for our happiness. Finally, for Schleiermacher, although God must not be thought of as deliberating or choosing before acting, nevertheless Christian religious self-consciousness truly ascribes intention to God, in the sense that God's love and wisdom are the motive and order of the divine causality.

These seven theologians make differing claims about what is designed by God. Athanasius seems to believe that design extends to everything which is an object of God's providence, including the number of hairs on a head. Maximus affirms design in the basic patterns of things, but grants that details of particular

individuals may be conditioned by their modes of
existence. Augustine is somewhat ambivalent, but
certainly believes that design extends to all the major
kinds of living things. Aquinas maintains that species
are created according to pre-existent ideas, but allows
for the operation of chance in producing individual
differences. Luther and Calvin both assert that
nothing happens without God's deliberate will, so that
every detail of every living thing is presumably
ordained by God. Schleiermacher also believes that
God's causality is absolute, but he is more reluctant
than his predecessors to draw consequences from this
which could conflict with the findings of natural
science.

All seven theologians, however, agree unanimously
on at least two points: (1) God's will, plan, idea, or
intention for the world is eternal and unchanging, and
(2) human beings are the main object of that will,
plan, idea, or intention. The principal ground of this
latter belief seems to be twofold: faith that God
became incarnate in a real human body and soul, and
faith that God can be trusted to act for our benefit.
All seven theologians are convinced that the
incarnation is willed, planned, designed, or intended
by God eternally, which means, at least from our
temporal perspective, before the human species actually
appeared on the earth. God did not merely await the
outcome of natural processes, and then become incarnate
in some suitable organism, but directed those processes
to produce an intended result. Furthermore, all seven
theologians would agree that we ought to trust God
completely, but this is possible only if God is both
absolutely powerful and absolutely loving, and if we

are the object of God's special concern. These
conditions cannot be fulfilled by fate, or chance, or
impersonal natural laws. On the contrary, they imply
that not only the existence of things in general, but
also the specific form of our existence, is willed,
planned, designed, or intended by God.

It is important to note that a search for the
argument from design in the thought of these seven
theologians would not have turned up anything like the
wealth of material that has been presented here. The
writings of most of them contain almost nothing that
could reasonably be construed as a proof of God's
existence based on design. Even in the writings of
Aquinas, arguments to design are far more prominent
than teleological proofs, which are only mentioned
twice. Clearly, the argument to design is a much more
integral part of the Christian theological tradition
than the argument from design.

Hodge's argument to design, though it differs in
some respects from some of the forms of the argument
found in these seven theologians, does not seem to
represent a significant departure from them. Hodge's
conviction that Christian belief in God necessarily
entails design in living organisms, particularly in the
human species, thus appears to be continuous with the
mainstream theological traditions of all major branches
of Christianity. It remains to be seen whether this
apparent continuity may be brought into serious
question by various criticisms of his theology.

(3) Criticisms of Hodge's Theology

Not surprisingly, Hodge attracted a fair amount of
theological criticism in his own day. After the close

of the nineteenth century, however, although Princeton
theology continued to develop in the hands of his
successors there were very few studies devoted to
Hodge's theology per se until the 1950's (two notable
exceptions being works by Danhof, 1929, and Nelson,
1935).[53] From the 1950's to the 1970's, a burgeoning
interest in nineteenth-century American religious and
intellectual history produced a number of studies
dealing with Hodge. Of these, some are primarily
historical treatments which attempt to give a more or
less balanced assessment of Hodge's theology in its
historical context; while others, usually written from
the standpoint of liberal Protestant theology, tend to
be decidedly more polemical. In response to these
latter treatments, a number of studies defending Hodge
have appeared in the 1980's. What follows is not
intended, of course, to be a review of everything which
has ever been written about Hodge, nor even a complete
discussion of every criticism which has been or could
be made of Hodge's theology, but merely a brief
examination of the most common criticisms, to determine
whether they weaken or invalidate Hodge's implicit
claim to be representing mainstream Christianity in his
critique of Darwinism.

At least one of Hodge's contemporaries criticized
him for relying too heavily on philosophy, but it was
not until the middle of the twentieth century that
scholars generally identified this philosophy as
Scottish common-sense realism. The principal reason
for the delay, perhaps, is that virtually all
nineteenth-century American intellectuals took the
Scottish philosophy for granted, and a clear
recognition of its pervasiveness awaited observers

further removed from its influence. In any case,
modern commentators seem to be unanimous in their
judgment that Hodge presupposed, and failed to realize
the extent to which he presupposed, Scottish common-
sense realism. These same commentators agree that in
this respect Hodge was no different from most of his
contemporaries in the United States, though they
disagree over the consequences the philosophy had for
Hodge's theology. Some claim that his thinking was so
"saturated" by it that his supposedly biblical theology
was biblical only for those who shared his
presuppositions, and that he derived "most" of his
knowledge of God from natural reason. Others would
consider these criticisms exaggerated, and argue that
Hodge's theology "was in no way a metaphysical system"
and retained its "fidelity" to scripture and the
Reformed confessions.[54]

According to Hodge's critics, two features of
Scottish common-sense philosophy directly affect his
critique of Darwinism: the absolute distinction between
mind and matter, which Hodge assumes in his objection
that Darwinism makes unintelligent matter do the work
of mind; and the principle that intelligence in the
cause can be deduced from design in the effect, which
Hodge assumes in his use of the argument from design.[55]
On the first point, it is true that Hodge uses the
mind/matter distinction in criticizing materialistic
and deistic theories of evolution; but he finally
rejects such theories primarily on the grounds that
they deny God's providential government of secondary
causes, a doctrine which he derives not from Scottish
philosophy but from scripture and the Westminster
Confession. Furthermore, Hodge's central objection to

Darwinism is not its denial of providence but its exclusion of design; and although his argument <u>from</u> design in Volume I of *Systematic Theology* is undeniably influenced by the principles of common-sense realism, the argument <u>to</u> design which constitutes the core of his critique appears to be derived from the Christian theological tradition rather than the Scottish philosophical tradition. Therefore, it is difficult to see how Hodge's reliance on Scottish philosophy in other matters would render his central objection to Darwinism unrepresentative of the Christian tradition as a whole.

A second common criticism levelled at Hodge's theology is that it follows more in the tradition of Turretin than of Calvin and the Westminster Confession. Critics point out that Turretin's theology neglected the need for the Holy Spirit and over-emphasized the power of human reason in attaining to knowledge of God's existence and attributes, and thus "breathed a very different spirit" from that of Calvin and Westminster.[56] Like the influence of Scottish philosophy, the influence of Turretin's theology on Hodge is undeniable, though again commentators disagree about the extent of that influence. Hodge's theistic proofs are similar to Turretin's, and Hodge does little to correct Turretin's neglect of the Holy Spirit. On the other hand, Hodge gives more prominence to revelation in his doctrine of creation than Turretin did in his, and Hodge does not hesitate to reject Turretin's doctrine of concursus as scholastic rather than biblical.[57]

The similarity between the theistic proofs of Turretin and Hodge does not weaken the latter's critique of Darwinism, just as the influence of Scottish philosophy does not weaken it, because the critique rests on the argument to design rather than the proof of God's existence from design. Hodge's relative neglect of the Holy Spirit may mean that his doctrine of how we know God is closer to Turretin's than to Calvin's; but Hodge's belief that God's existence entails design in living organisms does not depend on this doctrine. One issue on which Hodge and Turretin happen to agree, namely the stability of species, does play a role in Hodge's critique; but, again, his argument to design is independent of this issue.[58] Therefore, the similarities between Hodge and Turretin would not warrant a claim that Hodge's central theological objection to Darwinism is representative only of seventeenth-century Calvinist scholasticism.

A third common criticism is related to the first two, though it is not reducible to them. Some of Hodge's contemporaries, as well as some modern critics, have charged him with holding an overly rationalistic view of faith. They claim that Hodge, unlike the Reformers, considers faith an intellectual assent to propositions based on external evidence, rather than a trusting commitment to God based on internal religious experience. According to one modern critic, Hodge's theology is not "faith seeking understanding," but moves instead from understanding to faith.[59] Hodge's defenders, however, consider these charges exaggerated. They argue that Hodge emphasizes the rational aspect of faith primarily in opposition to Schleiermacher and the mystics, but that when confronting rationalists he relies on faith in scripture and on religious experience. Furthermore, according to one defender,

knowledge for Hodge (like knowledge for Calvin) is not
just intellectual but involves the whole person.[60]

Is Hodge's argument to design overly rationalistic?
The implicit first premise, that God's existence
entails design in living organisms, is apparently
assumed on the basis of the doctrines of creation and
providence. In his treatment of these doctrines in
Systematic Theology, Hodge does argue to design, but he
does so primarily on the basis of scripture, not
reason. On the other hand, the implicit second premise
(in the modus ponens form of the argument), that God
exists, is derived by Hodge at least partly from
rationalistic proofs in *Systematic Theology*.[61] In this
respect, Hodge may very well be more rationalistic than
the Reformers, or perhaps even the pre-Reformation
tradition. Nevertheless, this rationalistic aspect of
Hodge's theology does not affect the first premise or
the conclusion: although Hodge establishes the second
premise by more rationalistic methods than Luther and
Calvin, all three agree that God's existence entails
design in the creation. Since they also agree on God's
existence, though they may argue for it in different
ways, they all agree on the conclusion that living
organisms are designed. Therefore, despite the
rationalistic cast which Hodge gives to the second
premise, his overall argument remains continuous with
the older tradition.

A fourth common criticism of Hodge's theology,
again related to the previous criticisms but not
reducible to them, concerns his understanding of
scripture. Some critics charge Hodge with holding a
mechanical view of inspiration, by which scripture is
considered to be inerrantly dictated by the Holy Spirit

with virtually no human input, but most commentators
would agree that this charge is inaccurate and unfair.
Some critics charge that Hodge departed from the
Christian tradition by claiming that the Bible is a
source of propositional truths about nature and
history, though others maintain that in this respect
Hodge " was neither unique nor innovative."[62]

If Hodge's critique of Darwinism had rested on a
fundamentalist interpretation of Genesis, it would
perhaps be relevant here to attempt to adjudicate these
conflicting evaluations of his view of scripture.
Issues which typically interest biblical
fundamentalists, however, such as the chronology and
other details of the Genesis creation narratives, play
little or no part in Hodge's critique. The first
premise of Hodge's argument to design depends on his
doctrines of creation and providence. He derives these
doctrines primarily from scripture, but they and their
implications for design are common to all major
branches of the Christian tradition. Therefore, even
if it could be shown that Hodge's understanding of
scripture were faulty or untraditional, his central
objection to Darwinism would be largely unaffected.

A fifth common criticism is that Hodge is simply
too polemical and too unwilling to entertain new ideas.
According to one recent critic, the "gravest charge"
against Hodge's theology is that it is "not so much an
approach to be discussed as a position to be defended,"
and others cite Hodge's own claim that no new idea
originated at Princeton Seminary during his tenure
there.[63] To whatever extent these charges are true,
however, they tend only to confirm Hodge's continuity
with the tradition: Athanasius, Maximus, and Augustine

developed their theologies at least partly in opposition to heretical challenges, and Luther and Calvin took polemical stands not only against the Roman Catholic Church but also against other reformers; and if no new ideas originated at Princeton it was because Hodge tried to remain faithful to Westminster Calvinism. Therefore, although Hodge's polemical attitude and resistance to new ideas may help to explain why he opposed Darwinism so vehemently, they do nothing to weaken the continuity between his central theological objection to Darwinism and the rest of the Christian tradition.

It seems, then, that the criticisms which are commonly levelled at Hodge's theology do not significantly affect his premise that Christian belief in God entails the claim that living organisms (or, at the very least, human beings) are designed. Since the Bible provides at least prima facie grounds for the claim, and since prominent representative theologians from the major branches of Christianity make similar claims, it seems reasonable to conclude that Hodge speaks not only for his own brand of American Calvinism, but also for mainstream Christianity as a whole, at least up through the nineteenth century. This is not to say that all people who consider themselves Christian would necessarily agree with Hodge on this point; but if they disagree, it is they who depart from the mainstream Christian tradition, and not Hodge.

Therefore, the first premise in Hodge's argument to design, that God's existence entails design in living organisms, can be considered broadly representative of traditional Christian belief. It remains to be seen, of course, whether the second premise in his critique, that Darwinism denies design, is an adequate characterization of Darwin's theory.

NOTES

1.   Dupré, *A Dubious Heritage*, 153, 158; McPherson, *Argument From Design*, 1-9; O'Grady, "Evolutionary Theory and Teleology," 563-565; Woodfield, *Teleology*, 1-18.

2.   Kelsey, *Uses of Scripture in Recent Theology*, 1-10, 158-216.

3.   The scripture quotations contained herein are from the Revised Standard Version of the Bible, copyrighted 1946, 1952, 1971 by the Division of Christian Education of the National Council of Churches of Christ in the U.S.A., and used by permission.

4.   Leith, *Creeds of the Churches*, 30-33.

5.   Florovsky, "Idea of Creation in Christian Philosophy,"66-67; Meyendorff, *Christ in Near Eastern Thought*, 99. See also Basil, "Hexaemeron," 5.9, 8.7-8.8, 9.2 (in *Letters and select Works*); Florovsky, "Idea of Creation in Christian Philosophy," 53-77; Quasten, *Patrology*, 20.

6.   Barth, *Protestant Theology in the Nineteenth Century*, 425.

7.   Kelly, *Early Christian Doctrines*, 226-247; Pelikan, *Christian Tradition* 1:173, 191-205; Tsirpanlis, "Aspects of Athanasian Soteriology," 25-40.

8.   Athanasius, "Discourses Against the Arians," 1.29, 3.62 (all references to works by Athanasius are in *Select Works and Letters*). See also Florovsky, "St. Athanasius' Concept of Creation," in *Collected Works of George Florovsky* 4:49-60; Wolfson, *Philosophy of the Church Fathers* 1:227-228.

9.   Athanasius, "On the Incarnation of the Word," 2; Athanasius, "Discourses Against the Arians," 3.61-3.65, 1.35-1.36, 2.76-2.78; Athanasius, "Against the Heathen,"4. See also Meijering, *Orthodoxy and Platonism in Athanasius*, 11-13, 102-103.

10. Athanasius, "Discourses Against the Arians,"
2.64,1.26, 2.24; Athanasius, "Defense of the Nicene
Definition,"7-9; Athanasius, "Discourses Against the
Arians," 2.25. See also Athanasius, "Against the
Heathen," 42, 46; Quasten, *Patrology*, 66-67;Meijering,
Orthodoxy and Platonism in Athanasius, 88.

11. Athanasius, "Discourses Against the Arians," 2.25;
Athanasius, "Against the Heathen," 2-3; Athanasius,
"Discourses Against the Arians," 2.75-2.78;Athanasius,
"On the Incarnation of the Word," 8-18.See also
Athanasius, "Discourses Against the Arians," 2.47-2.49;
Florovsky, "Idea of Creation in Christian Philosophy,"
72-73; Tsirpanlis,"Aspects of Athanasian Soteriology,"
34-39.

12. Athanasius, "Discourses Against the Arians," 2.19.

13. Origen, "De Principiis," 2.1.1. See also
Florovsky,"Idea of Creation in Christian Philosophy,"
60-63; Kelly, *Early Christian Doctrines*, 180-182;
Meyendorff, *Byzantine Theology*, 132-134; Origen, "De
Principiis,"2.10.6.

14. Florovsky, *Collected Works*, 4:61; Florovsky, "Idea
of Creation in Christian Philosophy," 63-65, 73-74;
Meyendorff, *Byzantine Theology*, 131-134; Meyendorff,
Christian Eastern Christian Thought, 100-101; Sherwood,
in Maximus, *The Ascetic Life. The Four Centuries on
Charity*, 46-47; Sherwood, *Earlier Ambigua*, 165-176;
Thunberg, *Microcosm and Mediator*, 81, 96-97, 100-101.

15. Meyendorff, *Byzantine Theology*, 140-142; Sherwood,
in Maximus, *The Ascetic Life. The Four Centuries on
Charity*, 52-53; Thunberg, *Microcosm and Mediator*, 100-
104.

16. Meyendorff, *Byzantine Theology*, 160; Meyendorff,
Christ in Eastern Christian Thought, 105-106, 114;
Thunberg, *Microcosm and Mediator*, 457; Tsirpanlis,
"Aspects of Maximian Theology of Politics, History, and
the Kingdomof God, 5-7.

17. *New Catholic Encyclopedia*, s.v. "Manichaeism".

18. Augustine, "Two Souls: Against the Manichaeans,"
6.9 (in *Writings Against the Manichaeans and Against
the Donatists*); Augustine, *Eighty-three Different
Questions*, q.46; Augustine, *On the Trinity*, 4.1;
Augustine, *Homilies on the Gospel of John*, 1:17.See

also Augustine, *On the Trinity*, 4.10; Augustine, *Literal Meaning of Genesis*, 2.6,2.8, 4.24, 4.32, 5.12, 5.15, 5.18; Augustine, *Free Choice of the Will*, 2.16; D'Arcy, "Philosophy of St. Augustine,"185-190; Gilson, *Christian Philosophy of Saint Augustine*, 197-199; TeSelle, *Augustine The Theologian*, 208-214.

19.   Augustine, "Of True Religion," 18.35 (in Earlier Writings); Augustine, *Literal Meaning of Genesis*, 5.21-5.22; Augustine, *Homilies on the Gospel of John*, 1:15; Augustine, *Literal Meaning of Genesis*, 6.15. See also Augustine, "On the Nature of Good: Against the Manichaeans," 30 (in *Writings Against the Manichaeans and Against the Donatists*); Augustine, *Literal Meaning of Genesis*, 3.14, 6.11; Augustine, *Free Choice of the Will*, 2.17.

20.   Augustine, *Letters*, 14; Augustine, *Eighty-three Different Questions*, q. 46. See also Augustine, *Literal Meaning of Genesis*, 5.20; Augustine, "Of True Religion," 18.35; O'Toole, *Philosophy of Creation in the Writings of St. Augustine*, 96-100; McKeough, *Meaning of the Rationes Seminales in St. Augustine*, 54, 57.

21.   Augustine, *Literal Meaning of Genesis*, 5.4, 5.5, 5.20-5.23, 6.1-6.11, 6.14-6.18.

22.   Gilson, *Christian Philosophy of Saint Augustine*, 206-208; McKeough, *Meaning of the Rationes Seminales in St. Augustine*, viii-x, 29-64, 95-110; O'Toole, *Philosophy of Creation in the Writings of St. Augustine*, 50, 70-102; Portalie, *Guide to the Thought of Saint Augustine*, 138-141; TeSelle, *Augustine the Theologian*, 216-219;

23.   Copleston, *Aquinas*, 9-13; McInerny, *St. Thomas Aquinas*, 17-34, 114-120.

24.   Aquinas, *Summa Theologica* Ia, q. 15, art. 1; q. 44, art. 3. See also Copleston, *History of Philosophy*, vol. 1, pt. 1, 188-205; vol. 1, pt. 2, 35-45.

25.   Aquinas, *Summa Contra Gentiles*, bk. 1, chaps. 54, 51; Aquinas, *Truth*, q. 3, art. 5. See also Aquinas, *Summa Theologica* Ia, q. 44, arts. 2-3; Copleston, *Aquinas*, 147-148; Henle, *Saint Thomas and Platonism*, 357-371; McInerny, *St. Thomas Aquinas*, 114-120.

26. Aquinas, *Summa Theologica* Ia, q. 15, art. 1;
Aquinas, *Truth*, q. 3, art. 1; Aquinas, *Summa Theologica*
Ia, q. 19, art. 4; Aquinas, *Summa Contra Gentiles*, bk.
1, chap. 72, art. 6. See also Aquinas, *Summa Theologica*
Ia, q. 14, arts.8-9; Aquinas, Truth, q. 2, art. 14;q.
23, art. 1; Aquinas, *On the Power of God*, q. 3, art.
15; Gilson, *A Christian Philosophy of St. Thomas
Aquinas*, 123-127; McInerny, *St. Thomas Aquinas*, 114-
115;.

27. Aquinas, *Summa Theologica* Ia, q. 34, art. 3;
Aquinas, *Truth* q. 4, art. 1; Aquinas, *Commentary on the
Gospel of St. John* 65.

28. Aquinas *Summa Contra Gentiles*, bk. 1, chap. 53,
art.5; Aquinas, *Summa Theologica* Ia, q. 14, art. 6;
Aquinas *Summa Contra Gentiles*, bk. 1, chap. 53, art. 5;
Aquinas, *Summa Theologica* Ia, q. 15, art. 2; q. 14,
art. 9. See also Aquinas, *Truth*, q. 3, art. 2; Aquinas
Summa Contra Gentiles, bk. 2, chaps. 39-45; Aquinas, *On
the Power of God* q. 3, art. 16; Aquinas, *Summa
Theologica* Ia, q. 11, art. 4; q. 14, arts. 1-9; q. 47,
arts. 1-2; Gilson, *Christian Philosophy of St. Thomas
Aquinas*, 123-127, 152-154; Garrigou-Lagrange, The
Trinity and God the Creator 354-356, 415-422; Geiger,
"Les Idees Divines Dans L'Oeuvre de S. Thomas," 206-
208; Henle, *Saint Thomas and Platonism*, 357-371;

29. Aquinas, *Summa Contra Gentiles*, bk. 2, chap. 39;
Aquinas, *Summa Theologica* Ia, q. 90, arts. 2-4; q. 91,
art.3; q. 93, arts. 1-7. See also Adler, *Problems for
Thomists: The Problem of Species*, 32-51.

30. Dillenberger, ed., Martin Luther, xiv-xxxiii.

31. Althaus, *Theology of Martin Luther*, 129; Althaus,
"Schöpfungsgedanke bei Luther," 3, 7-8; Lofgren,
Theologieder Schöpfung bei Luther, 52.

32. Luther, *Works* 1:36, 22:8-12, 13:91-92, 17:29,
1:36; See also Luther, *Works* 1:49, 52:42; Lofgren,
Theologie der Schopfung bei Luther, 28-29, 50, 69.

33. Luther, *Works* 22:26-29, 17:118. See also Luther,
Works 11:11-16, 11:338-339;

34. Althaus, "Schöpfungsgedanke bei Luther," 3-5;
Althaus, *Theology of Martin Luther*, 105-11; Lofgren,
Theologie der Schöpfung bei Luther, 25, 38-43, 58-60;

158

Prenter, *Spiritus Creator*, 193-195; Watson, *Let God be God*, 79.

35. Luther, *Works* 11:15, 1:36-47. See also Luther, *Works* 14:344, 22:29, 22:91; Lofgren, *Theologie der Schöpfung bei Luther*, 63, 67-68, 77-78; Watson, *Let God be God*, 79.

36.Luther, *Works* 1:36-56, 1:80-84.See also Luther, *Works* 1:104, 1:119, 11:15, 28:183-196; Lofgren, *Theologie der Schöpfung bei Luther*, 63, 67-69, 77-78.

37. Calvin, *Institutes of the Christian Religion*, bk. 1, chap. 5, sec. 1; chap. 14, sec. 20; Calvin, *Commentary on Hebrews* 11:3; Calvin, *Institutes of the Christian Religion*, bk. 1, chap. 5, sec. 14; chap. 6, sec. 1; chap. 5, sec. 9; chap. 14, sec. 20. See also Calvin, *Commentary on Acts* 17:27; Dowey, *Knowledge of God in Calvin's Theology*, 238-241; Niesel, *Theology of Calvin*,39-51; Wendel, *Calvin*, 160-165.

38. Calvin, *Institutes of the Christian Religion*, bk. 1, chap.14, sec. 20; Calvin, *Commentary on Genesis* 1:26; Calvin, *Commentary on Acts* 17:26; Calvin, *Commentary on Hebrews* 11:3; Calvin, *Institutes of the Christian Religion*, bk.1, chap. 16, sec. 6; Calvin, *Commentary on Psalms* 8:6; Calvin, *Institutes of the Christian Religion*, bk. 1, chap.14, secs. 2, 22. See also Calvin, *Institutes of the Christian Religion*, bk. 1, chap. 15, sec. 3; bk. 1, chap.16, sec. 2; Niesel, *Theology of Calvin*, 63-68; Torrance, *Calvin's Doctrine of Man*, 23-26, 38-46, 68-70; Wendel, *Calvin*, 176.

39. Calvin, *Institutes of the Christian Religion*, bk. 1, chap.16, sec. 3; chap. 5, sec. 4; chap. 18, sec. 1; chap. 16, sec. 4; chap. 17, sec. 6; chap. 16, secs. 3, 5,8,9; chap. 17, secs. 2, 7. See also Calvin, *Commentary on Hebrews* 11:3; Calvin, *Commentary on Acts* 17:26-28; Calvin, *Institutes of the Christian Religion*, bk. 1, chap.16, secs. 1-9;bk. 1, chap. 18, secs. 1-3; Klaaren, *Religious Origins of Modern Science*, 40-44; Wendel, *Calvin*, 177-180.

40. Calvin, *Institutes of the Christian Religion*, bk. 1, chap.10, sec. 2; Calvin, *Commentary on the Gospel According to John* 1:3.

41. Redeker, *Schleiermacher: Life and Thought*, 149; See also Ebeling, "Schleiermacher's Doctrine of Divine Attributes," 127-128, 146, 169; Redeker,

Schleiermacher: Life and Thought, 108-116, 149-154; Williams, *Schleiermacher the Theologian*, 169.

42. Schleiermacher, *Christian Faith*, pars. 3, 4, 11. See also Schleiermacher, *Speeches on Religion*, 48-50, 90-95, 101; Schleiermacher, *On the Glaubenslehre*, 38.

43. Schleiermacher, *Christian Faith*, par. 30; Schleiermacher, *On the Glaubenslehre*, 70; Schleiermacher, *Christian Faith*, par. 16 (postscript), par. 30.1-30.3, par. 34.1-35.3, par. 167.1. See also Barth, *Protestant Theology in the Nineteenth Century*, 455-457; Niebuhr, "Schleiermacher and the Names of God," 184-187; Redeker, *Schleiermacher: Life and Thought*, 114; Williams, *Schleiermacher the Theologian*, 81-83.

44. Schleiermacher, *Christian Faith*, pars. 36, 39, 41; Schleiermacher, *On the Glaubenslehre*, 67; Schleiermacher, *Christian Faith*, par. 40; Schleiermacher, *On the Glaubenslehre*, 60-61; Schleiermacher, *Christian Faith*, par.38. See also Brandt, *Philosophy of Schleiermacher*, 242; Redeker, *Schleiermacher: Life and Thought*, 122-123; Thiel, *God and World in Schleiermacher's Dialektik and Glaubenslehre*, 176-187.

45. Schleiermacher, *Christian Faith*, pars. 46-47.

46. Schleiermacher, *Christian Faith*, pars. 51-54; Schleiermacher, *On the Glaubenslehre*, 48-50. See also Ebeling, "Schleiermacher's Doctrine of Divine Attributes," 129-148; Gerrish, *Prince of the Church*, 59-60, 64; Niebuhr, *Schleiermacher on Christ and Religion*, 240-245; Redeker, *Schleiermacher: Life and Thought*, 109, 115, 119-121; Thiel, *God and World in Schleiermacher's Dialektik and Glaubenslehre*, 156-160; Williams, *Schleiermacher the Theologian*, 90-92.

47. Schleiermacher, *Christian Faith*, par. 168. See also Brandt, *Philosophy of Schleiermacher*, 248-251.

48. Schleiermacher, *Christian Faith*, par. 41, pars. 54-55. See also Ebeling, "Schleiermacher's Doctrine of Divine Attributes," 142-143; Niebuhr, "Schleiermacher and the Names of God," 178, 191-195, 204; Williams, *Schleiermacher the Theologian*, 94-95.

49. Schleiermacher, *On the Glaubenslehre*, 57; Schleiermacher, *Christian Faith*, pars. 164-168. See

also Ebeling, "Schleiermacher's Doctrine of Divine Attributes," 149-160; Gerrish, *Prince of the Church*, 64-67; Niebuhr, "Schleiermacher and the Names of God," 188-192; Pauck, "Schleiermacher's Conception of History," 46; Williams, *Schleiermacher the Theologian*, 87, 113, 170-176.

50. Schleiermacher, *Christian Faith*, par. 164, par. 168. See also Niebuhr, *Schleiermacher on Christ and Religion*, 245-247; Redeker, *Schleiermacher: Life and Thought*, 123.

51. Brandt, *Philosophy of Schleiermacher*, 251.

52. Niebuhr, "Schleiermacher and the Names of God," 191-192.

53. Danhof, *Charles Hodge as a Dogmatician*; Nelson, *Rise of the Princeton Theology*.

54. Ahlstrom, "Theology in America," 263-265; Dabney, "Hodge's Systematic Theology," 168; Johnson, "Attitudes of the Princeton Theologians," 16-22; Noll, *Princeton Theology*, 33-35; McAllister, "Nature of Religious Knowledge," 181-183, 287-288, 294, 304-306; Rogers & McKim, *Authority and Interpretation*, 289; Vander Stelt, *Philosophy and Scripture*, 144.

55. Vander Stelt, *Philosophy and Scripture*, 122; Johnson, "Attitudes of the Princeton Theologians," 85.

56. Rogers & McKim, *Authority and Interpretation*, 279-281. See also Ahlstrom, "Theology in America," 262-266; Danhof, *Charles Hodge as a Dogmatician*, 175, 184-187; Loetscher, *Broadening Church*, 21; McAllister, "Nature of Religious Knowledge," 348; MacGregor, "Dr. Charles Hodge and the Princeton School," 462.

57. Beardslee, "Theological Development at Geneva," 167-168, 172-174, 259, 262-263, 313-314, 371-372, 429-430,717; Hoffecker, *Piety and the Princeton Theologians*, 70.

58. Beardslee, "Theological Development at Geneva," 265.

59. McAllister, "Nature of Religious Knowledge,"340-341. See also Bozeman, *Protestants in an Age of Science*, 171, 209; Dabney, "Hodge's Systematic Theology," 168-181; Danhof, *Charles Hodge as a*

Dogmatician, 183; Lindsay, "Doctrine of Scripture,"
278-282; Loetscher, *Broadening Church*, 21-22;
McAllister, "Nature of Religious Knowledge," 271, 310-
322, 327-330, 342-347; Nelson, "Rise of the Princeton
Theology," 342; Rogers & McKim, *Authority and
Interpretation*, 295; Sandeen, *Roots of Fundamentalism*,
118.

60.   Hoffecker, *Piety and the Princeton Theologians*,
64-68, 71, 77-80;Nelson, "Rise of the Princeton
Theology," 318,342.

61.   Charles Hodge, *Systematic Theology*, 1:565-568,
581-586.

62.   Balmer, "The Princetonians and Scripture," 364.
See also Balmer, "The Princetonians and Scripture,"
354-355; Danhof, *Charles Hodge as a Dogmatician*, 56-60;
Dillenberger, *Protestant Thought and Natural Science*,
234-236; Hoffecker, *Piety and the Princeton
Theologians*, 59; Johnson, "Attitudes of the Princeton
Theologians," 33; Lindsay, "Doctrine of Scripture,"
278-282; McAllister, "Nature of Religious Knowledge,"
292-308, 325-326, 331-339; Noll, *Princeton Theology*,
41-43; Rogers & McKim, *Authority and Interpretation*,
282-292; Sandeen, Roots of Fundamentalism, 124;
Sandeen, "Princeton Theology," 314; Schaff, *Theological
Propaedeutic*, 392; Woodbridge, "Does the Bible Teach
Science?" 202, 205.

63.   Sandeen, *The Roots of Fundamentalism*, 130. See
also Ahlstrom, "Theology in America," 264-265; Danhof,
Charles hodge as a Dogmatician, 43; MacGregor, "Hodge
and the Princeton School," 466-467; McAllister, "Nature
of Religious Knowledge," 375; Noll, *Princeton Theology*,
38-39; Patton, "Charles Hodge," 363; Rogers & McKim,
Authority and Interpretation, 276-277.

CHAPTER FIVE
The Second Premise: Darwinism and the Denial of Design

The second premise of Hodge's critique is that Darwinism excludes design. Hodge distinguishes between (1) theories of evolution which, though naturalistic, do not exclude design, and (2) Darwin's particular theory, which (he claims) does. The two categories are similar in certain respects: an advocate of either (1) or (2) might believe in a divine origin of the evolutionary process; both (1) and (2) claim that, once initiated, the process is autonomous, neither requiring nor admitting any further divine activity; and neither (1) nor (2) necessarily make any claims in favor of design. The difference is that theories in category (1) posit a mechanism which is consistent with design, but Darwin's theory posits a mechanism which is not. Theories in (1), though naturalistic or deistic, are a-teleological: they are silent with respect to design, but they do not exclude it. According to Hodge, however, Darwin's theory posits a mechanism which is sufficiently random to be characterized as anti-teleological: not only is it silent with respect to design, but also logically excludes it.

According to several twentieth-century writers, Hodge misinterpreted Darwin's theory in this respect.[1] If he did, of course, then his central theological objection is erroneous. Hodge might still object to

Darwinism on other grounds, but on his own terms he
could not characterize it as atheism. Therefore,
evaluating the soundness of Hodge's argument involves
asking whether, or in what senses, Darwin's theory
excludes design.

It is helpful to recall that design carries several
different meanings. In particular, it is important to
distinguish what aspects of the world can be said to be
designed. For example, design can extend to one or
more of the following: the tendency of bodies to act
for ends, the general order of the universe, the major
kinds of living organisms, each species of animal or
plant, or every detail of every living thing. It may
be that Darwin's theory is compatible with one or more
of these, in which case Hodge would be mistaken in
claiming that Darwinism excludes all teleology. On the
other hand, if Darwin's theory excludes design in even
one sense that follows necessarily from Christian
belief in God, Hodge would be correct in claiming
that, from a Christian viewpoint, Darwinism is atheism.

In what sense or senses, then, does Darwinism
exclude design? Any attempt to answer this question
must first tackle the difficulty of defining Darwinism:
just as some people may describe themselves as
Christians even though they are thoroughly
untraditional in one or more of their beliefs, so it is
possible for people to call themselves Darwinians even
though they significantly modify Darwin's theory in one
or more respects. Nevertheless, this does not mean
that Darwinism, any more than Christian belief, must be
regarded as completely amorphous.

The difficulty of defining Darwinism is aggravated
by the widespread tendency to confuse Darwin's

particular theory with both philosophical and biological evolution in general. In an attempt to dispel some of the confusion, one twentieth-century writer has suggested restricting "Darwinian" to "those propositions and implied assumptions which may properly be ascribed to a source in the *Origin*," and using "Darwinistic" to describe all other views, including Lamarckian evolution and Spencerian philosophy.[2] The following analysis, however, need not limit itself to the *Origin of Species*, and uses the terms "Darwinism" and "Darwinian" to refer to Darwin's theory as presented in three of his published works (all of them read by Hodge): *On the Origin of Species*, *The Descent of Man*, and *The Variation of Animals and Plants Under Domestication*. Furthermore, since the following analysis is not concerned with non-Darwinian evolutionary views (except to exclude them from the discussion), it refers to such views and their adherents by the terms "evolutionism," "evolutionary," and "evolutionist" to minimize confusion. Finally, since the term "Darwinist" has recently been used by one writer to distinguish non-Darwinian evolutionists from Darwinians,[3] "Darwinist" is not used at all in the following discussion. For the sake of clarity, adherents are referred to either as Darwinians or as evolutionists.

Narrowing the focus to Darwin's theory as presented in his major published works is analogous to identifying the scriptures and the early ecumenical creeds as the normative texts for Christian belief; but just as the scriptures and the creeds alone could not settle the issue of design for Christianity, so Darwin's published works cannot settle the issue for

Darwinism. Deducing the logical consequences for
design from Darwin's theory may be fraught with as many
difficulties as defining mainstream Christian belief on
the basis of scripture. It could be argued that in the
century since Darwin a professional network of
Darwinian biologists has more or less defined an
orthodoxy analogous to the orthodoxy defined by the
Christian theological tradition, and that certain
prominent biologists could be selected to represent
that orthodoxy; but that network existed only in
incipient form in Hodge's day, and it seems a bit
unfair, or at least anachronistic, to evaluate his
understanding of Darwinism on the basis of opinions
which emerged long after he died. It is possible,
however, to identify certain prominent interpreters of
Darwin's theory who lived and wrote during Hodge's
lifetime, and whose interpretations could shed
considerable light on the teleological implications of
Darwinism.

Therefore, just as mainstream Christian belief was
defined, for the purpose of this analysis, on the basis
of scripture, the ecumenical creeds, and the views of
representative theologians up to the nineteenth
century, so Darwinism can be defined by certain
normative texts and certain representative nineteenth-
century interpreters. To make the parallel complete,
the following analysis also examines the views of some
critics who maintain that Hodge's critique is based on
a misinterpretation of Darwin's theory.

(1) Normative Texts

Although the only relevant issue here is design, it
seems appropriate to summarize Darwin's theory as it is

presented in the three texts read by Hodge, before
referring to the few passages in them which explicitly
discuss design.

In the *Origin of Species*, Darwin lists several
factors that he believes are responsible for the
production of new species. The first is variation:
"under changing conditions of life organic beings
present individual differences in almost every part of
their structure." A second is inheritance, through
which organisms characterized by certain variations
will "tend to produce offspring similarly
characterized." The third is a "severe struggle for
life" due to the fact that "many more individuals are
born than can possibly survive." The fourth factor is
the principle by which variations favorable to survival
are preserved, while unfavorable ones are destroyed;
and "this principle of preservation, or the survival of
the fittest," Darwin calls "natural selection".[4]

According to Darwin, "many laws regulate variation,
some few of which can be dimly seen." These include
direct and indirect effects of "the conditions of
life", the effects of "the use or disuse of parts", and
"correlation", by which Darwin means that variations in
one part of an organism may be linked to variations in
another. Only variations which are inheritable are
important for his theory, though "the laws governing
inheritance are for the most part unknown." Why a
particular variation is sometimes inherited and
sometimes not, "no one can say," but it is clear from
domestic breeding that variations can often be
transmitted through many generations.[5]

Darwin notes that "a struggle for existence
necessarily follows from the high rate at which all

organic beings tend to increase." Since similar
organisms, dependent on the same food or environmental
conditions, must compete with each other for limited
resources, the struggle for life is "most severe
between individuals and varieties of the same species."
Under such circumstances, "individuals having any
advantage, however slight, over others, would have the
best chance of surviving and of procreating their
kind." On the other hand, "any variation in the least
degree injurious would be rigidly destroyed." This
"natural selection," which Darwin compares to the
conscious selection of the domestic breeder, "leads to
the improvement of each creature in relation to its
organic and inorganic conditions of life." Given a
sufficient number of generations, Darwin believes that
"the small differences distinguishing varieties of the
same species steadily tend to increase, till they equal
the greater differences between species of the same
genus, or even of distinct genera." Once life was
"originally breathed by the Creator into a few forms or
into one," the "production of the higher animals" would
then directly follow from the laws of variation,
inheritance, the struggle for life, and natural
selection.[6]

In the *Variation of Animals and Plants Under
Domestication*, Darwin reiterates his conviction that
"species have generally originated by the natural
selection, not of abrupt modifications, but of
extremely slight differences." The natural laws
governing the origin of these differences are largely
unknown, but include the changing conditions of life,
use and disuse, and correlation. Extrapolating from
the evidence of domestic breeding, Darwin concludes

that "not only the various domestic races, but the most distinct genera and orders within the same great class, -- for instance, whales, mice, birds, and fishes, -- are all the descendants of one common progenitor." Under the influence of natural selection, "each slight modification of structure which was in any way beneficial under excessively complex conditions of life, will have been preserved, whilst each which was in any way injurious will have been rigorously destroyed. And the long-continued accumulation of beneficial variations will infallibly lead to structures as diversified, as beautifully adapted for various purposes, and as excellently coordinated, as we see in the animals and plants all around us. Hence I have spoken of selection as the paramount power, whether applied by man to the formation of domestic breeds, or by nature to the production of species."[7]

Although Darwin noted in the *Origin of Species* that by this theory "light will be thrown on the origin of man and his history," in the *Descent of Man* he explicitly extends his conclusions to the human species: "man incessantly presents individual differences in all parts of his body and in his mental faculties. These differences or variations seem to be induced by the same general causes, and to obey the same laws as with the lower animals. In both cases similar laws of inheritance prevail. Man tends to increase at a greater rate than his means of subsistence; consequently he is occasionally subjected to a severe struggle for existence, and natural selection will have effected whatever lies within its scope." According to Darwin, this scope includes the evolution from lower animals of not only the human body, but also "mental powers" and "moral qualities".[8]

Both the *Origin of Species* and the *Descent of Man* contain occasional references to the notions of chance and design. In the *Origin of Species*, Darwin explains that although he sometimes speaks of variations as if they were due to chance, this is "a wholly incorrect expression, but it serves to acknowledge plainly our ignorance of the cause of each particular variation." Similarly, he believes that the notion of design often serves as a confession of ignorance: "It is so easy to hide our ignorance under such expressions as the 'plan of creation,' 'unity of design,' &c., and to think that we give an explanation when we only restate a fact." In the *Descent of Man*, Darwin's concluding summary contains the following carefully worded passage: "The birth both of the species and of the individual are equally parts of that grand sequence of events, which our minds refuse to accept as the result of blind chance. The understanding revolts at such a conclusion, whether or not we are able to believe that every slight variation of structure, the union of each pair in marriage, the dissemination of each seed, and other such events, have all been ordained for some special purpose."[9]

In the *Variation of Animals and Plants Under Domestication*, Darwin concludes with a much lengthier discussion of the implications of his theory for the notion of design. Using the metaphor of a house built by an architect using uncut fragments of stone found "at the base of a precipice," Darwin explains that "the fragments of stone, though indispensable to the architect, bear to the edifice built by him the same

relation which the fluctuating variations of each
organic being bear to the varied and admirable
structures ultimately acquired by its modified
descendants." The shape of each fragment "may be
called accidental, but this is not strictly correct;
for the shape of each depends on a long sequence of
events, all obeying natural laws." Nevertheless, "in
regard to the use to which the fragments may be put,
their shape may be strictly said to be accidental." In
Darwin's metaphor, of course, the architect is natural
selection.[10]

The accidental character of variations leads to "a
great difficulty," and although Darwin acknowledges
that in attempting to face it he is "travelling beyond"
his "proper province," he elaborates its implications:
"An omniscient Creator must have foreseen every
consequence which results from the laws imposed by Him.
But can it be reasonably maintained that the Creator
intentionally ordered, if we use the words in any
ordinary sense, that certain fragments of rock should
assume certain shapes so that the builder might erect
his edifice? If the various laws which have determined
the shape of each fragment were not predetermined for
the builder's sake, can it with any greater probability
be maintained that He specially ordained for the sake
of the breeder each of the innumerable variations in
our domestic animals and plants; -- many of these
variations being of no service to man, and not
beneficial, far more often injurious, to the creatures
themselves? Did He ordain that the crop and tail-
feathers of the pigeon should vary in order that the
fancier might make his grotesque pouter and fantail
breeds? Did He cause the frame and mental qualities of

the dog to vary in order that a breed might be formed
of indomitable ferocity, with jaws fitted to pin down
the bull for man's brutal sport? But if we give up the
principle in one case, -- if we do not admit that the
variations of the primeval dog were intentionally
guided in order that the greyhound, for instance, that
perfect image of symmetry and vigour, might be formed,
-- no shadow of reason can be assigned for the belief
that variations, alike in nature and the result of the
same general laws, which have been the groundwork
through natural selection of the formation of the most
perfectly adapted animals in the world, man included,
were intentionally and specially guided." If we assume
that they were, then "the plasticity of organisation,
which leads to many injurious deviations of structure,
as well as that redundant power of reproduction which
inevitably leads to a struggle for existence, and, as a
consequence, to the natural selection or survival of
the fittest, must appear to us superfluous laws of
nature. On the other hand, an omnipotent and
omniscient Creator ordains everything and foresees
everything. Thus we are brought face to face with a
difficulty as insoluble as that of free will and
predestination."[11]

These passages reveal several elements of Darwin's
theory which bear on its implications for design:(1)
natural selection, or survival of the fittest, is the
paramount power responsible for producing the different
adaptations which characterize species, genera, and
orders; (2) a second essential factor is variation,
which results from the operation of natural laws but
which is not intentionally guided. These elements form
the basis for the interpretations which follow.

(2) Representative Interpreters

Like the theologians chosen to represent the various branches of the Christian tradition, representative interpreters of Darwinism should be chosen on the basis of their prominence and influence, rather than because they happen to hold a particular doctrine. Of the Darwinians who lived and wrote during Hodge's lifetime, the most prominent and influential was of course Charles Darwin himself. A logical second choice would be Thomas Henry Huxley, "Darwin's bulldog" and ardent defender, who did more than any other individual at the time to represent and interpret Darwin's theory to the world. Darwin and Huxley, then, can be taken to represent the inner circle of English Darwinians who constituted the first major "branch" of the Darwinian tradition.

One group of prominent nineteenth-century interpreters rejected both Darwinism and traditional Christianity. People in this group typically advocated, as their mature position, some form of non-Darwinian evolution and some form of unorthodox religious belief. The group included biologist Alfred Russel Wallace, the co-discoverer of natural selection, and author Samuel Butler, a prominent critic of Darwin's theory.[12] Since people in this group explicitly repudiated "orthodox" Darwinism, however, it seems unfair to select them to interpret it. Likewise, it would be unfair to choose interpreters from among those who (like Hodge) rejected Darwinism while remaining orthodox Christians. This latter group included Hodge's colleague, Princeton College President James McCosh, who readily embraced the notion of biological evolution and even accepted some elements of Darwin's theory, but who substantially modified the theory and even explicitly repudiated it when it came to the origin of sensation, instinct, intelligence and morality.[13] Just as the representatives of Christianity were chosen from the ranks of committed Christians, so the interpreters of Darwinism should be chosen from the ranks of those who considered themselves committed Darwinians.

Among those who did consider themselves committed to Darwinism, there was one nineteenth-century group which could be considered a second major "branch" of the tradition. People in this group not only defended Darwin's theory, but also continued to defend orthodox Christianity. These "Christian Darwinians," as they have been called, included James Iverach and Aubrey Moore in England, and Asa Gray and George Wright in the United States. Gray has been called "the foremost defender of Darwinism in America," and even the "Godfather of Darwinism."[14] Since Gray and Wright were Hodge's opponents in America, forming a partnership to convince Americans that Darwinism is compatible with Christianity, it is appropriate to have them represent this branch of the Darwinian tradition.

As interpreters of Darwinism, then, Darwin and Huxley can serve to represent the original inner circle, and Gray and Wright the Christian Darwinians. It is not the purpose of the following analysis to describe their views about every aspect of Darwinism, but only their views about its implications for design. Their personal religious beliefs, moreover, are dealt with only to the extent that they shed light on those implications.

(a) Darwin

Before turning directly to Darwin's views on design, it is worthwhile to deal with two preliminary matters. First, some scholars have questioned whether the views which Darwin expressed in public reflected his true opinions on religious issues. It has been pointed out that English law in the nineteenth century penalized atheists and materialists in various ways, and that Darwin was well aware of the adverse consequences which could attend the publication of opinions judged to be atheistic. Darwin even wrote to a friend in 1863 that he had "truckled to public opinion" by using "the Pentateuchal term of creation" in the *Origin of Species*, when all he had really meant was that primordial forms "appeared by some wholly unknown process." His "truckling" in this instance, however, does not necessarily mean that his statements about design were disingenuous. Although there is some evidence to warrant such a suspicion, there is also testimony from his family and friends that he was generally quite courageous and sincere in expressing his opinions, though he tried to avoid offending people in religious matters. For the purpose of this analysis, then, while recognizing that the circumstances may have induced Darwin to choose his words carefully, it can be assumed that his expressed views on design represented his true thoughts on the subject.[15]

Second, it is now well established that Darwin's personal religious views underwent significant modification during his lifetime. As a youth he believed in something approaching orthodox

Christianity, and even studied for the ministry. As he
grew older, he "gradually came to disbelieve in
Christianity," and became increasingly agnostic. The
development of Darwin's religious views would be
relevant here if it could be shown that his growing
disbelief were a consequence of the design implications
of his theory. Indeed, there are some indications that
this may have been the case: in his autobiography
Darwin acknowledges that "the old argument from design
in Nature, as given by Paley, which formerly seemed to
me so conclusive, fails, now that the law of natural
selection has been discovered." Even if Darwin's
agnosticism were really a consequence of his theory,
however, it may have been due as much to other factors
as to its implications for design. For example, it
excluded supernatural intervention in the evolutionary
process, and it implied that the convictions of the
human mind, which has been developed from the mind of
the lower animals, are untrustworthy. Given the
difficulty of isolating such factors, the following
analysis does not attempt to trace the development of
Darwin's thinking, but focuses primarily on Darwin's
opinions about design during the 1860's and 1870's.[16]

His basic position is the one he takes in the
Variation of Animals and Plants Under Domestication:
natural selection is the paramount power, but it merely
preserves beneficial variations and eliminates harmful
ones; variations are due to natural laws, many of them
unknown, but they are undirected in the sense that they
arise without any regard for the welfare of the
organism or the progress of evolution; and although the
mind cannot conceive of the universe as the product of
chance, the assumption of an omnipotent and omniscient

creator would imply that all its details are designed, but the undirected character of natural selection and variation seems to contradict this assumption. Darwin reiterates this position many times in his personal letters. Natural selection is analogous to domestic selection, but unlike the latter its only purpose is survival: the organs which it produces "have been formed so that their possessors may compete successfully with other beings, and thus increase in number." Furthermore, just as Darwin could not regard "each variation in the rock-pigeon, by which man has made by accumulation a pouter or fantail pigeon, as providentially designed for man's amusement," so he could "see no reason why he should rank the accumulated variations by which the beautifully adapted woodpecker has been formed, as providentially designed." As a result, the detailed design on which Paley based his argument disappears: "We can no longer argue that, for instance, the beautiful hinge of a bivalve shell must have been made by an intelligent being, like the hinge of a door by man. There seems to be no more design in the variability of organic beings, and in the action of natural selection, than in the course which the winds blows."[17]

According to Darwin, neither natural selection nor variation, the two major elements of his theory, provides an opening for design. Although he compares natural selection to an architect, he repeatedly denies that he intends to attribute conscious agency to it. He repudiates the anthropomorphic connotations which many of his contemporaries associate with the selection metaphor, insisting that he uses it only "as a geologist does the word denudation -- for an agent,

expressing the result of several combined actions."
Since natural selection is powerless without
variations, which arise independently of it, he
sometimes wishes he had used the term "natural
preservation"; but by the time the confusion became
obvious, the former term was "so largely used abroad
and at home that I doubt whether it could be given up."
In addition to this negative reason for retaining the
term, Darwin has positive reasons as well: natural
selection is analogous to artificial selection not only
in its dependence on variations, but also in the
impressiveness of its results. Natural selection
solves the problem of how organisms become adapted to
the conditions of life, "as artifical selection solves
the adaptation of domestic races for man's use."
Furthermore, the former is more efficient than the
latter: a domestic breeder "scarcely selects except
external and visible characters, and secondly, he
selects for his own good; whereas under nature,
characters of all kinds are selected exclusively for
each creature's own good." Darwin can thus see "no
limit to the perfection of the coadaptations which
could be effected by Natural Selection." It is still
the case, however, that "natural selection means only
the preservation of variations which independently
arise."[18]

In what senses, then, could natural selection be
said to produce designed results? One twentieth-
century study of Darwin's own views on the subject
concludes that there are at least three such senses:
natural selection (1) will always produce adaptation of
the organism to its environment, (2) will never produce
in an organism structures that are harmful to it, and

(3) will never produce structures in one organism solely for the benefit of another. Since these can legitimately be regarded as "purposes," it would be incorrect to say that Darwin considers natural selection totally purposeless. On the other hand, natural selection does seem to exclude the claim that specific organs or organic forms are designed. According to Darwin, not even organs of sight or the order of primates, much less the human eye or the human species, could be considered designed results of natural selection.[19]

Darwin also denies that variations, the second major element in his theory, could lead to designed results. His reasons for this denial are scientific, philosophical, and theological. The first category includes the observation that the vast majority of variations are useless or harmful rather than beneficial. It thus makes no sense to Darwin to say that variations are designed: if someone says "God ordained that at some time and place a dozen slight variations should arise, and that one of them alone should be preserved in the struggle for life and the other eleven should perish in the first or few first generations, then the saying seems to me mere verbiage. It comes to merely saying that everything that is, is ordained." The second category of reasons includes the philosophical assumption that naturalistic science is competent to investigate and explain the origin of species. The idea that "each variation has been providentially arranged seems to me to make Natural Selection entirely superfluous, and indeed takes the whole case of the appearance of new species out of the range of science." The third category includes

Darwin's conviction that designing each slight
variation would be beneath God's dignity and contrary
to God's benevolence. Referring once again to the
breeding of domestic pigeons, Darwin notes that "it
seems preposterous that a maker of the universe should
care about the crop of a pigeon solely to please man's
silly fancies." Furthermore, "I cannot persuade myself
that a beneficent and omnipotent God would have
designedly created the Ichneumonidae with the express
intention of their feeding within the living bodies of
Caterpillars, or that a cat should play with mice. Not
believing this, I see no necessity in the belief that
the eye was expressly designed."[20]

Darwin reasons that unless all variations are
designed, none of them are. If the "interposition of
the Deity" is uncalled for in the case of domestic
variations, he could "see no reason whatever for
believing in such interpositions in the case of natural
beings." Or "if anything is designed, certainly man
must be," but Darwin "cannot admit that man's
rudimentary mammae...were designed," therefore (by
implication) man is not designed. Such all-or-nothing
reasoning seems to be based primarily on Darwin's
commitment to naturalistic explanation: either the
origin of species can be explained in exclusively
naturalistic terms, or it cannot really be explained at
all. Darwin writes that he "would give absolutely
nothing for the theory of Natural Selection, if it
requires miraculous additions at any one stage of
descent." To a lesser extent, his reasoning may have
been based on his understanding of the idea of God: if
the deity were going to pre-ordain any details, then an
omnipotent and omniscient deity would presumably pre-

ordain all; but a wise and benevolent deity would not
ordain many of the details which are actually observed;
therefore (by implication), no details are pre-
ordained. Whatever the basis, Darwin's reasoning leads
him to conclude that all variations are undesigned.[21]

Darwin nevertheless maintains that variations are
due to natural laws. Since he acknowledges that many
of these laws are unknown, it would seem to be possible
for each variation to be completely pre-determined by
natural causes; and his theory is sometimes interpreted
as being deterministic in this sense.[22] If this
interpretation were correct, it would be possible to
maintain that the course of evolution was predetermined from the beginning. Darwin's theory, though
incompatible with a theistic notion of providential
design, would nevertheless be compatible with a deistic
notion of deterministic design: it would not exclude
the possibility that even though the laws of evolution
are autonomous, God pre-programmed them to produce
exactly those forms of living things which have
actually emerged. It seems very unlikely, however,
that Darwin would agree with this interpretation.
Although by "chance" he sometimes means only that the
causes of variation are largely unknown (leaving open
the question of determinism), he sometimes means that
their causes involve an irreducible element of
uncertainty, at least with respect to their function in
evolution. His metaphor of the stone house in the
Variation of Animals and Plants Under Domestication is
the classic statement of this view. Although it is
"not strictly correct" to call the shape of the
fragments of stone accidental, since their shape
"depends on a long sequence of events, all obeying

natural laws," yet "in regard to the use to which the fragments may be put, their shape may be strictly said to be accidental." Referring to this passage years later, he explains that "the only way I have used the word chance," at least in its strict sense, has been "in relation to the variations of organic beings having been designed," or (in other words) "in relation only to purpose in the origination of species."[23] One recent study of Darwin's notebooks concludes that despite his ambivalent use of the word "chance" he is convinced that the relation of variability to evolutionary improvement is basically a random affair.[24] Darwin thus rejects deterministic design as well as providential design.

This does not mean, however, that Darwin is willing to attribute every aspect of evolution to chance. He repeatedly affirms his "inward conviction" that "the Universe is not the result of chance." Although he distrusts this conviction, since he believes that the human mind is descended from the minds of lower animals, he appears to be genuinely persuaded of "the extreme difficulty or rather impossibility of conceiving this immense and wonderful universe" as "the result of blind chance or necessity." This puts him in "a simple muddle; I cannot look at the universe as the result of blind chance, yet I can see no evidence of beneficent design, or indeed of design of any kind, in the details." Although he fears that the issue may ultimately be incomprehensible, he is "inclined to look at everything as resulting from designed laws, with the details, whether good or bad, left to the working out of what we may call chance."[25]

This last statement is probably the best summary of
Darwin's mature position on design. Although it is
likely that he never resolved the question of ultimate
purpose to his own satisfaction, he at least believed
that his theory does not exclude all design: someone
could embrace Darwinism and yet consistently maintain
that natural laws, including the laws of variation and
natural selection, are designed. According to Darwin's
own understanding of the theory, however, specific
details are due to chance, not merely in the sense that
their causes are unknown but in the sense that they are
really accidental. Neither of the two major elements
in the theory can be plausibly interpreted as directed:
not variation, because it is predominantly useless or
harmful; and not natural selection, because its only
function is to insure that the few survivors of the
struggle for life will be better able to withstand the
next round. If evolution is really due to these two
factors, then the particular forms taken by organisms,
species, genera, and orders are accidental. Therefore,
Darwin's version of Darwinism excludes the possibility
that any specific form of life is designed. In
particular, it implies that human beings, as the latest
products of an inherently directionless process, must
be regarded as undesigned.[26]

(b) Huxley

Darwin preferred to avoid public controversy,
especially on religious issues, but Huxley apparently
thrived on it. His combativeness not only earned him
the nickname, "Darwin's bulldog," but also contributed
significantly to the prevalence of the warfare
metaphor.[27] He devoted relatively little attention,

however, to the issue of design. Of the theological
issues in the Darwinian controversies, the conflicts
between evolution and Genesis cosmogony and between
naturalism and biblical supernaturalism attracted most
of his interest.[28] Nevertheless, he does have some
things to say about the design implications of Darwin's
theory.

According to Huxley, "the doctrine of Evolution is
the most formidable opponent of the commoner and
coarser forms of Teleology." Indeed, when he first
read the *Origin of Species* Huxley was struck by "the
conviction that Teleology, as commonly understood, had
received its deathblow at Mr. Darwin's hands."
According to common teleology, organs and adaptations
first appear fully grown and perfectly suited to the
needs of the organism: this view maintains that the eye
"was made with the precise structure which it exhibits,
for the purpose of enabling the animal which possesses
it to see." Darwin's theory replaces this notion with
the doctrine that organs and adaptations emerge
gradually from many slight modifications, none of which
is perfect but only relatively better than its
competitors. In other words, "for the notion that
every organism has been created as it is and launched
straight at a purpose, Mr. Darwin substitutes the
conception of something which may fairly be termed a
method of trial and error." Huxley illustrates the
difference with an analogy: "According to Teleology,
each organism is like a rifle bullet fired straight at
a mark; according to Darwin, organisms are like
grapeshot of which one hits something and the rest fall
wide."[29]

Nevertheless, "there is a wider Teleology, which is
not touched by the doctrine of Evolution, but is
actually based upon the fundamental proposition of
Evolution." This proposition is that all things are
the products of uniform natural laws. Huxley is
"disposed to think it the most important of all truths"
that "the cosmic process is rational" and that
"throughout all duration, unbroken order has reigned in
the universe." Furthermore, he maintains that "the
theological equivalent of the scientific conception of
order is Providence," which thus seems to him "far more
important than all the theorems of speculative
theology."[30]

Huxley's notion of a wider teleology appears, at
first glance, to correspond closely to Darwin's
admission that general laws may be designed even though
their detailed consequences are not. Consistent with
this apparent correspondence is a statement by Huxley
in a letter written in 1888: "If you break a piece of
Iceland spar with a hammer, all the pieces will have
shapes of a certain kind, but that does not imply that
the Iceland spar was constructed for the purpose of
breaking up in this way when struck." There is,
however, a significant difference between the positions
of the two men: for Huxley, the rational order of the
universe means "the total exclusion of chance from a
place even in the most insignificant corner of Nature."
All living organisms are the "result of the mutual
interaction, according to definite laws, of the forces
possessed by the molecules of which the primitive
nebulosity of the universe was composed." Therefore,
"the existing world lay potentially in the cosmic
vapour," and "a sufficient intelligence could, from a

knowledge of the properties of the molecules of that vapour, have predicted, say the state of the fauna of Great Britain in 1869." Huxley acknowledges that this is determinism, but he claims that "the doctrine of determinism follows as surely from the attributes of foreknowledge assumed by the theologian, as from the universality of natural causation assumed by the man of science."[31]

Do Huxley and Darwin really differ on this point, or is the difference only a matter of emphasis? In Huxley's interpretation, when Darwin speaks of chance or spontaneous variations "he merely means that he is ignorant of the cause of that which is so termed."[32] Some of Darwin's references to chance do indeed mean this; but Darwin goes on to say, in other contexts, that whatever the cause is, it produces variations which are truly accidental, while Huxley goes on to say that all natural causes produce results which are truly predetermined. The difference between Darwin's position and Huxley's could be compared to the difference between modern physics, with its statistical uncertainties, and traditional Newtonian mechanics.[33] Not only does Huxley differ from Darwin on this point, but he also, at least at first glance, appears to be inconsistent with himself. If evolution is deterministic, then it would seem to be unnecessary to make teleology wider rather than coarser: every detail would be completely predetermined by initial conditions in the "cosmic vapour". If the universe and its laws had been created by God, then in this interpretation God could have predetermined every detail of every organism, including the precise structure of every individual eye. Huxley even acknowledges that "the teleological and mechanical views of nature are not, necessarily, mutually exclusive;"[34] yet he explicitly repudiates the deistic kind of detailed design with which his deterministic view is compatible. The only consistent option seems to be that every detail is predetermined but totally purposeless, and Huxley is sometimes interpreted as holding this position;[35] but then why speak of teleology at all?

In fairness to Huxley, it must be admitted that teleology was not his central concern, except perhaps to the extent that he insisted on excluding final causes from scientific method.[36] In general, he was far more concerned with the purely scientific aspects of evolution, and when he did venture into the theological arena it was usually to combat biblical cosmogony and supernaturalism. Furthermore, Huxley did not have a faithful friend and correspondent who relentlessly prodded him to examine the implications of design -- unlike Darwin, who had Asa Gray.

(c) Gray

Asa Gray was already a renowned botanist by the time Darwin published his *Origin of Species*. Raised a Presbyterian, Gray became a Congregationalist when he joined the faculty at Harvard, and he remained a moderate Calvinist throughout his life. Like other Protestant naturalists in the first half of the nineteenth century, Gray was heavily influenced by natural theology, and the argument from design played an important part in his thinking. Unlike many of his contemporaries, however, he became convinced of the general notion of evolution even before 1859; and when the *Origin of Species* appeared, he immediately welcomed

it as an ally in his opposition to advocates of the
immutability of species, such as Agassiz.[37]

Agassiz attacked Darwin's theory as atheistic
because it claimed that species are derived from other
species by natural causes, rather than created
immutable by divine design. Gray argues that the
evolution of species by natural causes is neither
atheistic nor incompatible with design: it is not
atheistic because it merely claims that what was
previously thought to be accomplished by God "directly
and at once" was actually accomplished "indirectly and
successively;" and it is not incompatible with design
because design is inferred from the "evidence of
contrivance" in the results, not from whatever
mechanism produced those results. Gray concludes that
the argument from design "is just as good now, if we
accept Darwin's theory, as it was before that theory
was promulgated." At this stage in the discussion,
however, Gray is not yet dealing with the specific
mechanism proposed by Darwin, but only with the general
notion of evolution by secondary causes.[38]

When Gray does turn to Darwin's proposed mechanism,
he sees in it both an advantage and a disadvantage.
The advantage is that the Darwinian mechanism accounts
for the useless and harmful adaptations for which the
older teleology had no explanation. The disadvantage
is that the mechanism also accounts for useful
adaptations in a way that seems to exclude design.
Gray deals with this apparent exclusion of design by
arguing for designed variations.

Gray believes that since naturalists see design in
species, they are justified in seeing design in the
variations which give rise to species, especially since

the causes of variations are unknown. Thus "we should
advise Mr. Darwin to assume, in the philosophy of his
hypothesis, that variation has been led along certain
beneficial lines. Streams flowing over a sloping plain
by gravitation (here the counterpart of natural
selection) may have worn their actual channels as they
flowed; yet their particular courses may have been
assigned." Gray also compares variations to raindrops:
those which fall into the ocean "are as much without a
final cause as the incipient varieties which come to
nothing! Does it therefore follow that the rains which
are bestowed upon the soil with such rule and average
regularity were not designed to support vegetable and
animal life?" Gray does not insist, however, that all
variations must be designed: "the accidental element
may play its part in Nature without negativing design
in the theist's view." Indeed, the accidental element
in Darwin's theory is the basis of its advantage in
explaining useless or harmful adaptations. But useful
adaptations testify to design, and since natural
selection merely picks out variations which are
independently presented to it, the presence of design
in the result indicates that at least some variations
are designed.[39]

Darwin, of course, disagreed. He wrote to Gray
that he was "charmed" with the stream metaphor, but
could not believe that variation "has been led along
certain beneficial lines." Darwin thought that Gray,
to be consistent, would also have to believe "that the
tail of the Fantail was led to vary in the number and
direction of its feathers in order to gratify the
caprice of a few men." Underlying Darwin's rejoinder,
apparently, is his assumption that the uniformity of

natural law excludes supernatural intervention and thus dictates that either <u>all</u> variations are designed or <u>none</u> of them is. Since so many variations are useless or harmful, Darwin concluded that "it is illogical to suppose" that all variations are designed. It was in response to Gray's arguments that Darwin summarized his position as being "inclined to look at everything as resulting from designed laws, with the details, whether good or bad, left to the working out of what we may call chance."[40]

It was also in response to Gray that Darwin concluded his *Variation of Animals and Plants Under Domestication* in 1868 with the metaphor of the stone house: the text includes Darwin's statement that "however much we may wish, we can hardly follow Professor Asa Gray in his belief" that variations are directed. In his American review of the book, Gray took what Darwin called "a good slap" at the metaphor: according to Gray, the metaphor demands that "not only the fragments of rock (answering to variation) should fall, but the edifice (answering to natural selection) should rise, irrespective of will and choice!" In a letter to Darwin, however, Gray privately conceded that "I found your stone-house argument unanswerable in substance (for the notion of design must after all rest mostly on faith, and on accumulation of adaptations, etc.); so all I could do was to find a vulnerable spot in the shaping of it, fire my little shot, and run away in the smoke. Of course I understand your argument perfectly, and feel the might of it."[41]

Darwin's public repudiation of Gray's position was used by Hodge as proof of their fundamental disagreement over design. In the same year that Hodge

published *What Is Darwinism?*, however, Gray wrote a
review article for *Nature* in which he praised "Darwin's
great service to natural science in bringing it back to
Teleology: so that, instead of Morphology <u>versus</u>
Teleology, we shall have Morphology wedded to
Teleology." Darwin read the article and promptly wrote
to Gray: "What you say about Teleology pleases me
especially, and I do not think any one else has ever
noticed the point. I have always said you were the man
to hit the nail on the head."[42] Christian Darwinians
Aubrey Moore and George Frederick Wright interpreted
Darwin's appreciative comment as proof that "the
Darwinians themselves testify" to design.[43] Several
twentieth-century writers have interpreted the exchange
as evidence of Darwin's "muddle" over design, as
indicative of Gray's belief that Darwinism would serve
to "buttress" the argument from design, or as "the
benevolent tolerance of the victors" in Darwin's inner
circle following his repudiation of Gray on the design
issue.[44]

The historical context of Gray's remark, however,
shows that the issue was not primarily design. In
nineteenth-century biology, teleology and morphology
referred to two competing methodologies: the former,
following Georges Cuvier, explained organic structures
in terms of function, by studying the purpose they
serve in adapting an organism to its "conditions of
existence;" while the latter, following Etienne
Geoffroy St. Hilaire, explained them in terms of form,
by studying their resemblance to structures in other
species to discover a "unity of type." The former
method was unable to explain the resemblance between
homologous structures serving different functions, such

as a bear's foot and a human hand. The latter method, in contrast, seemed much more adaptable to the evolutionary notion of descent from a common ancestor. The growing popularity of evolutionary ideas thus led to a comparative neglect of the teleological method among biologists.[45]

Darwin believed that by accounting for structures as the products of both adaptation to the environment and descent from a common ancestor, his theory reconciled the two approaches. He writes in the *Origin of Species* that "on my theory, unity of type is explained by unity of descent. The expression of conditions of existence, so often insisted on by the illustrious Cuvier, is fully embraced by the principle of natural selection." Gray had seen the significance of Darwin's reconciliation as early as 1860, when he referred to the tension between teleology and morphology and concluded that "Mr. Darwin harmonizes and explains them naturally. Adaptation to the conditions of existence is the result of natural selection; unity of type, unity of descent."[46]

Morphologists as well as teleologists, however, tended to believe in design, though the morphological notion of design emphasized regularity of pattern, while the teleological notion emphasized utility. The apparent denial of design by Darwin's theory thus offended not only the teleologists but also many morphologists. Darwin's reconciliation of teleology and morphology, therefore, did not mean that he was promoting design, and was not interpreted that way by contemporary biologists. Otherwise, Huxley would not have written in a single paragraph that Darwinism is "entirely and absolutely opposed to Teleology, as it is commonly understood," and that "the apparently diverging teachings of the Teleologist and of the Morphologist are reconciled" by it.[47]

Therefore, to construe the 1874 exchange between Gray and Darwin on the relationship of morphology and teleology as indicating a reconciliation between them on the issue of design is seriously to misinterpret it. After Darwin's public repudiation of Gray's view in 1868, both men seem to have recognized that the gulf between them on this issue was unbridgeable. The two remained good friends, however, and the exchange dealing with morphology and teleology seems to have been conducted with genuine good humor: both were well aware that "teleology" meant both "design" and "functional method," and according to Gray's biographer "Gray knew he was making a joke when he said that Darwin had reintroduced teleology into natural history."[48]

Gray did not give up his attempts to interpret Darwinism so as to make it compatible with design, though he did give up trying to convert Darwin to his views. Furthermore, though he refused to concede that variations had been proven to be undesigned, he largely gave up arguing for designed variations. To some extent, Gray shifted his claim for design to natural selection, adopting the metaphor of a ship: "Natural selection is not the wind which propels the vessel, but the rudder which, by friction, now on this side and now on that, shapes the course. The rudder acts while the vessel is in motion, effects nothing when it is at rest. Variation answers to the wind." Before 1868, however, Gray had argued that design must be in the variations because it could not plausibly be attributed to natural selection; and even in 1880, speaking to a Yale audience about the evolution of higher life forms, the formation of organs, and the emergence of sensation and consciousness, Gray could "hardly conceive that any one should think that natural selection scientifically accounts for these phenomena."[49] Therefore, the shift of metaphorical emphasis from variation to natural selection was not very convincing, not even to Gray himself. Increasingly, he turned his attention to reformulating the argument from design.

Gray recognized that the argument from design can take several forms. For example, instead of starting from particular adaptations in living organisms, it can start from the general orderliness of the universe. Although he was not ready to concede that Darwinism eliminated the evidence on which the former rested, Gray shifted his emphasis to the latter, arguing that "faith in an order, which is the basis of science" cannot reasonably "be dissevered from faith in an Ordainer, which is the basis of religion." Since Darwin was ready to grant that the laws of evolution may have been designed even though the resulting details were not, there was no danger here of a conflict with Darwin's theory. In addition to the argument from order, Gray also began to develop an argument based on the directed behavior of living organisms, or what might be called an argument from ends. Neither of these was new, of course: although Gray may not have realized it, both of them were known to Aquinas.[50]

In advocating these various reformulations, Gray believed that "the important thing to do, is to develop a right evolutionary teleology," in order to satisfy

Christians that there is no less design in "Divine works effected step by step" than there is in instantaneous creation, and in order to convince "antitheistic people" that "without the implication of a superintending wisdom nothing is made out, and nothing credible."[51] This statement reveals the two most prominent elements in Gray's thinking: his determination to convince Christians that the general notion of evolution does not exclude design, and his concern to make the argument from design convincing to the growing number of his scientific colleagues who were not theists.

The first element had been prominent since 1859, when Gray had defended Darwin's theory against the anti-evolutionism of Agassiz. It was also prominent in his review of Hodge's *What Is Darwinism?* in 1874. According to Gray's reading of the book, Hodge's central objection to Darwinism is that it denies design by excluding divine intervention in the evolutionary process. Thus "interference proves to be the keynote of Dr. Hodge's system," and Gray devotes the bulk of his rebuttal to demonstrating the compatibility of theism with the general notion of evolution by secondary causes.[52] Gray thus misinterprets Hodge's position: he fails to see that Hodge's central objection is that the Darwinian mechanism excludes detailed design in the results of evolution. Just as Gray is unwilling to grant the validity of Darwin's anti-teleological interpretation of his theory, so he is unwilling or unable to see the full force of Hodge's critique.

The second most prominent element in Gray's thinking is the restructuring of the argument from design. Gray devoted considerable thought to the argument from design, not so much, perhaps, because his own religious faith depended on it, but because he saw it as a way to keep science religious. By restructuring the Paleyan form of the argument, and basing it on the general orderliness of the universe instead of on detailed adaptations in living organisms, Gray could defend it against the objections even of strict Darwinians. Gray was never satisfied with this reformulation, however, and his biographer suspects that "he may have been indulging in an element of wishful thinking" by proposing it. He continually sought instead to "re-establish the evidence of design on the basis it ought to stand upon." According to his biographer, Gray hoped to be remembered by future generations as "one of the few who fought manfully for the very citadel of natural theology when misguided friends were hurling away its bulwarks."[53]

In the course of his efforts to preserve natural theology, Gray realized more and more that no form of the argument from design is compelling to someone who chooses not to grant its conclusion, and that the conviction of design ultimately rests on religious faith. His own faith induced him to read design into Darwin's theory: first he read it into variations, because it seemed unlikely that natural selection could produce designed results; but when he felt the might of Darwin's stone house metaphor, he read design into natural selection. Through all this, he remained a Darwinian in the broad sense that he considered variation and natural selection to be the basic mechanisms of evolutionary change; but he never conceded Darwin's view that the mechanism is inherently unable to produce design in living organisms.[54]

(d) Wright

George Frederick Wright was a Congregationalist pastor and amateur geologist when he first read Asa Gray's articles about Darwinism. Within a decade, he had become professor of New Testament at Oberlin College and a leading authority on glacial geology. In the intervening years, he and Gray teamed up to defend Darwin's theory against theological opponents such as Hodge.[55]

Like Gray, Wright focused much of his attention on the relationship between theistic design and evolution through secondary causes. Wright maintains that it is not necessary for a theist to insist on divine intervention in natural processes to explain evolution. Since design is inferred from the complexity of the resulting adaptation, rather than the mode of its production, no explanation in terms of secondary cause can affect the inference. Thus "Darwinism does not disturb the argument for an intelligent designer, but pertains only to the times and modes in which the forces of design are introduced."[56]

Wright concedes, however, that Darwinism "modifies in some degree the interpretation of that design." Like Gray, he advocates an "extension of the Paleyan argument" to the general order of the universe. According to Wright, "we must endeavor to shift the point of view from that in which we see things singly and disconnected to a position from which they shall be seen as parts of an organic whole," since "God has taken more pains to reveal to us his methods and laws, than to reveal his particular ends."[57]

Having thus provided the grounds for reconciling theism with Darwin's view of evolution, Wright nevertheless argues for more: like Gray, he insists that Darwin's theory does not exclude the more traditional notion of design. Since variations are due to unknown causes, and natural selection is "so elastic," God can use the mechanism to produce detailed design: "we cannot tell deductively what variations will arise, unless we know all about the constitution of the individual, and all about the outward circumstances that act upon it to produce variation; and we cannot know what variations will be perpetuated till we know how each is related to the whole system of nature. It would seem that such an hypothesis left God's hands as free as could be desired for contrivances of whatever sort he pleased." In other words, the unknown complexities which Darwin believed to be inherently accidental, and which Huxley took to be completely determined but purposeless, Wright interpreted as due to God's providential activity.[58]

Wright knew very well, of course, that Darwin did not agree with him and Gray on this point. In addition, then, to reformulating the argument from design and insisting that the Darwinian mechanism left room for God's providential activity, Wright proposed several analogies between Darwinism and Calvinism. The main point of the analogies was to show that various difficulties in Darwin's theory resemble various difficulties in Calvinist theology. One of those difficulties concerns design: "the adjustment of the doctrines of foreordination and free-will occasion

perplexity to the Calvinist in a manner strikingly like
that experienced by the Darwinian in stating the
consistency of his system of evolution with the
existence of manifest design in nature." Like Darwin
himself, Wright thus compares the difficulty of
reconciling the Darwinian mechanism with design to the
difficulty of reconciling predestination with free
will. To some extent, Wright goes on to resolve the
tension by repeating his appeal to "a higher and more
comprehensive design," claiming that a Calvinist, like
a Darwinian, "might say a general system was designed"
without insisting on design in all its details. He
concludes that "if Darwinism appears to banish design
from nature, and to be fatalistic, it is only because
it is liable to the same class of misunderstandings
against which Calvinism has had so constantly to
contend."[59]

The curious feature of Wright's analogy is not his
characterization of Calvinism (a characterization with
which Calvin would not have agreed), but its implied
concession that Darwinism excludes detailed design.
Wright's reformulation of the argument from design is
independent of such detailed design, but does not
concede Darwin's exclusion of it. Wright's insistence
that the complexity of the Darwinian mechanism leaves
room for God's providential activity, if it is intended
to argue for anything at all, must be intended as an
argument for more detailed design than Darwin is
willing to concede. Yet, in his analogy with
Calvinism, Wright seems almost to grant Darwin's
interpretation.

As Wright grew older he began to have serious
doubts about the sufficiency of Darwin's theory. Like

Gray, he continued to be a Darwinian in a broad sense;
but by the turn of the century he explicitly denied
that Darwinism is sufficient to account for all of
evolution. Although it may explain how varieties
become species, and even how species become genera,
"Darwin's theory of the origin of species through
natural selection was not a theory of general
evolution." During the same period, Wright (who by
then was professor of New Testament at Oberlin) became
increasingly convinced that a Christian's faith in
design is independent of the argument _from_ design:
"Our inspiring hope is that we are moving along the
lines of development laid down by divine wisdom, and
made clear to us, not in the dim twilight of the
natural creation, but in the written history of the
chosen people, and by the continued illumination of Him
who is the light of the world."[60]

Wright, like Gray, thus seems to have moved closer
to an argument _to_ design in his later years. In the
prime of their partnership to defend Darwinism,
however, they both relied on an argument _from_ design,
reformulated on the basis of the general order of the
universe instead of particular adaptations. It is
interesting to note, in passing, that this raises a
problem for the received view of the nineteenth-century
Darwinian controversies. A corollary of the received
view is that reconciliation with Darwinism often took
the form of abandoning the argument from design. Yet
in America, Gray and Wright relied on a reformulated
argument from design as a major part of their strategy
of reconciliation. Although the brief survey of their
positions presented here is insufficient, by itself, to
justify a claim that they represent significant

counter-examples to the received view, the problem does seem to warrant further examination.

This observation must not, however, obscure the main point of this analysis. The central issue here is the adequacy of Hodge's second premise: in what senses does Darwinism deny design? The normative texts, and Darwin's own interpretation of them, lead to the conclusion that although the laws of nature may be designed, particular species are undesigned. Huxley interprets the theory in a completely deterministic sense, but likewise denies that particular species are designed, perhaps because the whole order of nature is undesigned. Gray and Wright reject Darwin's interpretation and read design into the theory, primarily in the form of directed variations.

This diversity of opinion, of course, makes it difficult to generalize about the implications of Darwin's theory for design. Although Darwin and Huxley maintain that the theory excludes the design of any particular species, Gray and Wright disagree. There are good reasons, however, for preferring Darwin's interpretation. The mere fact that he originated the theory does not necessarily make him the best interpreter of it, of course, but it does suggest that he devoted more thought to it than the other three. Furthermore, he was clearly more committed to the theory than he was to any notion of design, unlike Gray and Wright, who continually attempted to tailor the theory to their prior conviction that living organisms evidence design. Darwin was thus in a position to consider the design implications of his theory more dispassionately than Gray or Wright. On the other hand, Darwin was prodded by his friendship and correspondence with Gray to think more rigorously about design than Huxley, who focused his attention primarily on scientific issues and on biblical cosmogony and supernaturalism. In comparison with the other three representatives, then, Darwin stands out as the most likely to have reflected objectively and perceptively on the design implications of his theory.

Furthermore, Darwin's interpretation is reasonable. The theory includes two basic elements, variation and natural selection. If variations are designed, then either all of them are designed, or some of them are. If all of them are designed, then God must have designed the majority of them to be useless or harmful, which is absurd. If some of them are, then God is intervening in the course of natural processes, which takes the whole matter out of the realm of science and renders the theory useless. If natural selection is designed, then God must resort to preserving or destroying variations which arise independently of divine control, which means that God is not really God. It also means that design is limited to whatever enables an organism to survive, which hardly seems like an adequate notion of design at all. If evolution really is caused by the natural selection of accidental variations, then it seems unreasonable to regard its detailed results as designed. The reasonableness of this interpretation does not mean, of course, that it is the only possible one; but it does mean that it deserves more consideration than if it rested merely on Darwin's authority.

According to Darwin's interpretation, however, the details of living organisms, including the distinctions between species, genera, and orders, cannot be regarded

as designed by God. Therefore, if Darwin's
interpretation of his own theory is taken to be
normative, then Darwinism denies that human beings are
designed by God. On this point Hodge and Darwin agree,
though of course Darwin believes his theory to be true
and Hodge believes it to be false. Its exclusion of
design, however, and not its truth or falsity, is the
issue here.

Since all forms of the argument to design insist
that God's design extends at least to human beings,
Darwinism denies design in at least one sense which
brings it into conflict with the argument. The second
premise of Hodge's critique thus seems to be an
adequate characterization of Darwinism, or at least of
Darwin's interpretation of Darwinism. Nevertheless,
there are some critics who specifically charge Hodge
with having misinterpreted Darwin's theory in this
respect.

(3) Criticisms of Hodge's Interpretation

Although many twentieth-century writers have argued
that Darwinism does not deny design, only a few have
explicitly charged that Hodge misinterpreted Darwin by
claiming that it does.

According to one critic, Hodge "constantly pushes
his opponent too hard, forcing meanings upon his
expressions which Darwin would not have admitted." As
an example, this critic cites Hodge's analysis of
Darwin's view of variation in *What Is Darwinism?*:
Hodge concludes that "not intentional" is "precisely
what Darwin means when he says that species arise out
of accidental variations." The critic claims that
Hodge thereby misinterprets Darwin, who merely

"confessed ignorance as to the causes of variations."[61]
Darwin's own views, however, as expressed both in the
Variation of Animals and Plants Under Domestication and
in his letters, clearly support Hodge's interpretation
on this point. While Darwin sometimes uses "chance"
merely to indicate ignorance of causes, he also
sometimes uses it to indicate that those causes are
undirected.

Another critic maintains that Hodge mistakenly
"accepted Huxley's anti-teleological interpretation of
Darwinism as authoritative," and thereby mistakenly
concluded that Darwinism necessarily leads to
atheism.[62] It is true that Hodge quotes Huxley's
interpretation at some length in *What Is Darwinism?*,
but only after quoting Darwin's own interpretation from
the *Variation of Animals and Plants Under
Domestication*. Hodge also quotes other advocates of
Darwinism, and several of its opponents. It is not the
case, then, that Hodge rests his anti-teleological
interpretation of Darwinism entirely or even largely on
Huxley's view.

According to some critics, Hodge's conclusion that
Darwinism is atheism is actually based on a
misrepresentation of Gray's views. In *What Is
Darwinism?*, Hodge quotes Gray's statement that "the
proposition that the things and events in nature were
not designed to be so, if logically carried out, is
tantamount to atheism," and that if Darwinism claims
that events and their results are undirected and
undesigned, then Darwinism is atheistic. Critics point
out that Hodge omits the portion of Gray's statement
following the phrase, "tantamount to atheism." Gray
goes on to say that "since most people believe that

some [things and events] were designed and others were
not," we should not "stigmatize as atheistically
disposed a person who regards certain things and events
as being what they are through designed laws (whatever
that expression means), but as not themselves specially
ordained." In other words, Hodge ignores the fact that
Gray qualifies his statement in such a way as to
exonerate Darwinism (at least in his own mind) from the
charge of atheism.[63] It is undeniable that Hodge fails
to quote Gray's entire statement, and also fails to
deal explicitly with Gray's argument that by
acknowledging the possibility of designed laws Darwin's
theory avoids atheism. Hodge does confront this
argument briefly in his exposition of Huxley's views,
but dismisses the "distinction between a higher and
lower teleology" as being "of no account in this
discussion."[64] Since the "designed laws" argument
persuaded at least some thoughtful people that
Darwinism and teleology are compatible, it must be
acknowledged that Hodge's failure to take it more
seriously constitutes a fault in his critique.

It is largely a fault in Hodge's tactics, however,
and it does not invalidate the critique: while designed
laws may be adequate to show the compatibility of
Darwinism with some form of the argument _from_ design,
they are inadequate to show its compatibility with the
argument _to_ design. An argument _from_ design which
relies on the general order of the universe can be made
just as well with Darwin's theory as without it; but an
argument _to_ design which concludes that the human
species is designed can be made only if that theory is
repudiated. In this sense, Hodge is quite justified in

dismissing the distinction between higher and lower teleology as irrelevant to the discussion.

For the same reason, the most common criticism of Hodge's interpretation of Darwinism misses the point. Several critics point out that Hodge claims Darwinism "rejects all teleology" and denies "all design." To show that Hodge is mistaken on this point, one critic quotes Darwin's *Descent of Man* to the effect that "our minds refuse to accept as the result of blind chance" the "grand sequence of events" which gives rise both to individuals and to species;[65] but Darwin, even when he was not discounting such convictions on the grounds that the human mind was descended from the minds of lower animals, was convinced that his theory was incompatible with design in anything more than general laws. Another critic quotes Darwin's statement that he is "inclined to look at everything as resulting from designed laws, with the details, whether good or bad, left to the working out of what we may call chance."[66] These critics accurately represent Darwin's views: clearly, Hodge was mistaken in claiming that Darwinism excludes all design.

Nevertheless, although Hodge undeniably exaggerates the extent to which Darwin's theory excludes design, for the purpose of his critique his characterization remains adequate. The argument to design proceeds from God's nature and existence to the conclusion that human beings are specifically designed by God. The denial of design in particular results of the evolutionary process, which follows from Darwin's interpretation of Darwinism, entails a denial that human beings are designed. It is this denial of design, and not the possible compatibility of Darwin's theory with the

notion that God designed the general order of the
universe, which is relevant to the logic of Hodge's
critique. Hodge weakens the polemical impact of his
critique by exaggerating the denial of design by
Darwinism and thereby diverting attention from the
central issue, but his exaggeration does not invalidate
his conclusion.

Since the normative texts of Darwinism and Darwin's
own interpretation of it support Hodge's claim that
Darwinism denies design, at least in one essential
sense, and since criticisms of Hodge's interpretation
do not invalidate his claim, the adequacy of his second
premise is established. Since Hodge's first premise is
representative of mainstream Christian theology up to
and including Schleiermacher, the conclusion of Hodge's
argument is compelling for anyone who accepts this
theological tradition and Darwin's own interpretation
of Darwinism. If God exists, then human beings, at
least, are designed by God; Darwinism denies that human
beings are designed by God; therefore, Darwinism is
tantamount to atheism.

NOTES

1.   Foster, *Modern Movement in American Theology*, 48; Johnson, "Attitudes of the Princeton Theologians Toward Darwinism," 109-112.

2.   Peckham, *The Triumph of Romanticism*, 178.

3.   Moore, *Post-Darwinian Controversies*, 217-220.

4.   Darwin, *Origin of Species*, 160, 92, 160.

5.   Darwin, *Origin of Species*, 7-17.

6.   Darwin, *Origin of Species*, 74, 88, 92-93, 578-579.

7.   Darwin, *Variation of Animals and Plants Under Domestication*, 2:495-514.

8.   Darwin, *Origin of Species*, 578; Darwin, Descent of Man, 2:369-377.

9.   Darwin, *Origin of Species*, 165, 570; Darwin, *Descent of Man*, 2:378.

10.   Darwin, *Variation of Animals and Plants Under Domestication*, 2:514-515.

11.   Darwin, *Variation of Animals and Plants Under Domestication*, 2:515-516.

12.   Turner, *Between Science and Religion*, 1-7, 246-256.

13.   Illick, "Reception of Darwinism at the Theological Seminary and the College at Princeton," 234-243; Moore, *Post-Darwinian Controversies*, 245-250; Smith, "Calvinists and Evolution," 340-341.

14.   Moore, *Post-Darwinian Controversies*, 269, 280-283; McGiffert, "Christian Darwinism," 5, 63.

15.   F. Darwin, *Life and Letters of Charles Darwin*, 2:202-203. See also F. Darwin, Life and Letters of

Charles Darwin, 1:274-276; Gillespie, *Charles Darwin and the Problem of Creation*, 139; Gruber, *Darwin on Man*, 35-45, 201-213; Himmelfarb, *Darwin and the Darwinian Revolution*, 382-384; Manier, *Young Darwin and His Cultural Circle*, 159; Ospovat, "God and Natural Selection," 187; Young, *Darwin's Metaphor*, 111.

16. F. Darwin, *Life and Letters of Charles Darwin*, 1:278-279. See also F. Darwin, *Life and Letters of Charles Darwin*, 1:40-41, 1:282-285, 2:7; Darwin and Seward, *More Letters of Charles Darwin*, 1:154, 191, 395; Gillespie, *Charles Darwin and the Problem of Creation*, 134-145; Himmelfarb, *Darwin and the Darwinian Revolution*, 380-388; Mandelbaum, "Darwin's Religious Views," 363-378; Ospovat, *Development of Darwin's Theory*, 1-5; Ospovat, "God and Natural Selection," 169-170; Ruse, *Darwinian Revolution*, 180-184.

17. F. Darwin, *Life and Letters of Charles Darwin*, 1:280, 283-284, 278-279. See also Darwin and Seward, *More Letters of Charles Darwin*, 1:191-192.

18. Darwin and Seward, *More Letters of Charles Darwin*, 1:126; F. Darwin, *Life and Letters of Charles Darwin*, 2:138; Darwin and Seward, *More Letters of Charles Darwin* 1:271, 208, 128, 145; F. Darwin, *Life and Letters of Charles Darwin*, 2:217. See also F. Darwin, *Life and Letters of Charles Darwin*, 2:9, 110, 182; Darwin and Seward, *More Letters of Charles Darwin*, 1:154, 161, 193, 213, 388-389, 395; Gillespie, *Charles Darwin and the Problem of Creation*, 132; Young, *Darwin's Metaphor*, 101-110.

19. Ospovat, "God and Natural Selection," 185.

20. Darwin and Seward, *More Letters of Charles Darwin*, 1:194, 191; F. Darwin, *Life and Letters of Charles Darwin*, 2:97, 105. See also F. Darwin, *Life and Letters of Charles Darwin*, 1:283-284; 2:146, 170, 245, 267; Darwin and Seward, *More Letters of Charles Darwin*, 192-193, 321; Gillespie, *Charles Darwin and the Problem of Creation*, 125; Hull, *Darwin and His Critics*, 62-64; Mandelbaum, "Darwin's Religious Views," 369-370; Ruse, *Darwinian Revolution*, 250.

21. F. Darwin, *Life and Letters of Charles Darwin*, 2:97, 174, 7. See also Darwin and Seward, *More Letters of Charles Darwin*, 1:154; Gillespie, *Charles*

Darwin and the Problem of Creation, 121-122; Gruber, Darwin on Man, 211-212; Hull, *Darwin and His Critics*, 49-54.

22. Darwin, *Origin of Species*, 165-166; Darwin and Seward, *More Letters of Charles Darwin*, 1:194; Hull, *Darwin and His Critics*, 66; Huxley, "Reception of the 'Origin of Species'," in F. Darwin, *Life and Letters of Charles Darwin*, 553.

23. Darwin, *Variation of Animals and Plants Under Domestication*, 2:515; Darwin and Seward, *More Letters of Charles Darwin*, 1:395. See also F. Darwin, *Life and Letters of Charles Darwin*, 2:105, 245; Darwin and Seward, *More Letters of Charles Darwin*, 1:191.

24. Manier, *Young Darwin and His Cultural Circle*, 117-123. See also Gillespie, *Charles Darwin and the Problem of Creation*, 106; Himmelfarb, *Darwin and the Darwinian Revolution*, 348; Mandelbaum, "Darwin's Religious Views," 370.

25. F. Darwin, *Life and Letters of Charles Darwin*, 1:285, 282; Darwin and Seward, *More Letters of Charles Darwin*, 1:321; F. Darwin, *Life and Letters of Charles Darwin*, 2:105-106. See also F. Darwin, *Life and Letters of Charles Darwin*, 1:283-284; 2:97-98, 146, 169-170, 247; Darwin and Seward, *More Letters of Charles Darwin*, 1:395.

26. Bowler, *Evolution: History of an Idea*, 211; Ghiselin, *Triumph of the Darwinian Method*, 153-159; Gillespie, *Charles Darwin and the Problem of Creation*, 84; Gruber, *Darwin on Man*, 213; Hull, *Darwin and His Critics*, 65; Irvine, *Apes, Angels, and Victorians*, 108-111, 175; Mandelbaum, "Darwin's Religious Views," 369-374; Ospovat, *Development of Darwin's Theory*, 30-33, 61, 72-73, 84, 225-226; Ospovat, "God and Natural Selection," 188-193; Young, *Darwin's Metaphor*, 101-105.

27. Eiseley, *Darwin's Century*, 234-244; Moore, *Post-Darwinian Controversies*, 58-68.

28. For example, see Huxley's *Science and the Hebrew Tradition* and *Science and the Christian Tradition* (vols. 4 and 5 of Huxley, *Collected Essays*).

29. Huxley, *Collected Essays*, 2:109-110, 82-84. See also Huxley, "Reception of the 'Origin of Species'," in F. Darwin, *Life and Letters of Charles Darwin*, 1:554; L. Huxley, *Life and Letters of Thomas Henry Huxley*, 2:195-196.

30. Huxley, *Collected Essays*, 2:110; L. Huxley, *Life and Letters of Thomas Henry Huxley*, 3:218-219. See also Huxley, *Collected Essays*, 2:59; Huxley, "Reception of the 'Origin of Species'," in F. Darwin, *Life and Letters of Charles Darwin*, 1:554.

31. Huxley, "Reception of the 'Origin of Species'," in F. Darwin, *Life and Letters of Charles Darwin*, 1:553-557; L. Huxley, *Life and Letters of Thomas Henry Huxley*, 3:57, 218-219.

32. Huxley, "Reception of the 'Origin of Species'," in F. Darwin, *Life and Letters of Charles Darwin*, 1:553. See also Huxley, *Collected Essays*, 2:181-182; L. Huxley, *Life and Letters of Thomas Henry Huxley*, 1:328.

33. Manier, *Young Darwin and His Cultural Circle*, 120.

34. Huxley, *Collected Essays*, 2:112.

35. Bowler, *Evolution: History of an Idea*, 230.

36. Ellegard, "Darwinian Theory and Nineteenth-Century Philosophies of Science," 380-381.

37. Dupree, Asa Gray, 44-45, 220-221; McGiffert, "Christian Darwinism," 5-9, 25-26, 41-52; Moore, *Post-Darwinian Controversies*, 269-270.

38. Gray, Darwiniana, 84-86. See also Dupree, *Asa Gray*, 269-270, 288; Moore, *Post-Darwinian Controversies*, 207-209, 271-272.

39. Gray, Darwiniana, 148, 157, 154-155. See also Dupree, *Asa Gray*, 296-297; McGiffert, "Christian Darwinism," 208-209; Moore, *Post-Darwinian Controversies*, 274.

40. F. Darwin, *Life and Letters of Charles Darwin*, 2:80, 146, 170, 105.

41. Darwin, *Variation of Animals and Plants Under Domestication*, 2:516; F. Darwin, *Life and Letters of Charles Darwin*, 2:267; Gray, "Variation of Animals and

Plants Under Domestication," 236; J. Gray, *Letters of Asa Gray*, 2:562.

42. Gray, "Charles Robert Darwin," 81; F. Darwin, *Life and Letters of Charles Darwin*, 2:367.

43. Aubrey Moore, quoted in Moore, *Post-Darwinian Controversies*, 265; Wright, "Divine Method of Producing Living Species," 454.

44. Himmelfarb, *Darwin and the Darwinian Revolution*, 349; McGiffert, "Christian Darwinism," 205; Young, *Darwin's Metaphor*, 111.

45. Ospovat, *Development of Darwin's Theory*, 6-38; Russell, *Form and Function*, 1-88; Ruse, *Darwinian Revolution*, 148.

46. Darwin, *Origin of Species*, 253; Gray, *Darwiniana*, 52-53. See also Darwin and Seward, *More Letters of Charles Darwin*, 1:387; Dupree, *Asa Gray*, 358, 382; Gray, Darwiniana, 356-357; Ospovat, *Development of Darwin's Theory*, 115, 148-151; Russell, *Form and Function*, 234-235, 239.

47. Huxley, *Collected Essays*, 2:86. See also Huxley, *Collected Essays*, 2:109-110; Ospovat, *Development of Darwin's Theory*, 9, 22-23; Ospovat, "God and Natural Selection," 186; Russell, *Form and Function*, 241.

48. Dupree, *Asa Gray*, 382. See also F. Darwin, *Life and Letters of Charles Darwin*, 2:165; Darwin and Seward, *More Letters of Charles Darwin*, 1:160; de Beer, *Charles Darwin*, 169; Dupree, *Asa Gray*, 339-340; Ghiselin, *Triumph of the Darwinian Method*, 155-158; Moore, *Post-Darwinian Controversies*, 270, 276.

49. Gray, *Darwiniana*, 386; Gray, *Natural Science and Religion*, 73.

50. Gray, *Darwiniana*, 235; Gray, *Natural Science and Religion*, 92-93. See also Bowler, "Darwinism and the Argument From Design," 31-32; Dupre, *Dubious Heritage*, 152-153; Dupree, *Asa Gray*, 379; Himmelfarb, *Darwin and the Darwinian Revolution*, 390.

51. J. Gray, *Letters of Asa Gray*, 2:656.

52. Gray, *Darwiniana*, 276. See also Gillespie, *Charles Darwin and the Problem of Creation*, 112.

53. Dupree, Asa Gray, 376; J. Gray, *Letters of Asa Gray*, 2:658; Dupree, *Asa Gray*, 359-360. See also Gillespie, *Charles Darwin and the Problem of Creation*, 115.

54. Dupree, *Asa Gray*, 355, 377-382; Gray, *Natural Science and Religion*, 86-91, 106-109; McGiffert, "Christian Darwinism," 236-237, 251-255, 374; Moore, *Post-Darwinian Controversies*, 276-279.

55. McGiffert, "Christian Darwinism," 65-91; Moore, *Post-Darwinian Controversies*, 280-283.

56. Wright, "Concerning the True Doctrine of Final Cause or Design in Nature," 363. See also McGiffert, "Christian Darwinism," 281-282; Wright, "Debt of the Church to Asa Gray," 530; Wright, *Scientific Aspects of Christian Evidences*, 89-92, 112-113.

57. Wright, "Concerning the True Doctrine of Final Cause or Design in Nature," 363, 374, 383. See also McGiffert, "Christian Darwinism," 82-99, 223-226; Moore, *Post-Darwinian Controversies*, 289-291.

58. Wright, "Objections to Darwinism, and the Rejoinders of its Advocates," 687. See also Moore, *Post-Darwinian Controversies*, 291-292; Wright, *Scientific Aspects of Christian Evidences*, 93-94.

59. Wright, "Some Analogies Between Calvinism and Darwinism," 61, 67, 64, 76. See also McGiffert, "Christian Darwinism," 277-279, 294-295; Moore, *Post-Darwinian Controversies*, 294-297.

60. Wright, "The Evolutionary Fad," 303, 316.

61. Foster, *Modern Movement in American Theology*, 48; Hodge, *What Is Darwinism?*, 56. See also notes 23 and 24.

62. McGiffert, "Christian Darwinism," 120.

63. Hodge, *What Is Darwinism?*, 176; Gray, "Darwin and His Reviewers," *Atlantic Monthly*, October, 1860, reprinted in *Darwiniana*, 138. The critics are Johnson, "Attitudes of the Princeton Theologians Toward

Darwinism," 117; McGiffert, "Christian Darwinism,"
243-244.

64. Hodge, *What Is Darwinism?*, 84.

65. Hodge, *What Is Darwinism?*, 52, 71; Darwin,
Descent of Man, 2:378. The critic is Foster, *Modern
Movement in American Theology*, 48.

66. F. Darwin, *Life and Letters of Charles Darwin*,
2:105. The critic is Johnson, "Attitudes of the
Princeton Theologians Toward Darwinism," 110-111, 118.

CHAPTER SIX
The Conclusion:
Christianity or Darwinism?

According to the received view, the most fundamental theological objection to Darwinism in the nineteenth century was based on the argument from design. The most prominent anti-Darwinian theologian in America, however, based his objection on the argument to design. Charles Hodge believed in design because he believed in God, not in a God because he saw design.

Like virtually all of his contemporaries in the United States, Hodge was thoroughly conditioned by Scottish common-sense philosophy, which relied on a sort of introspective Baconian empiricism to discover intuitive truths in the human mind. Like his predecessor and mentor at Princeton Theological Seminary, Archibald Alexander, he was also trained in the rationalistic theological style of seventeenth-century Calvinist scholastic Francis Turretin. The major intellectual influence on him, however, was the Reformed Christianity of John Calvin and the Westminster Confession, which considered scripture to be the only reliable source of knowledge about God. Throughout his life Hodge did his utmost to remain faithful to the Calvinist tradition; he even boasted that no new ideas originated at Princeton Seminary during his tenure there, by which he meant no doctrines

not already found in Westminster Calvinism. Yet he
taught that interpretations of scripture ought not to
ignore scientific facts, and he was more progressive
than some of his contemporaries in adapting biblical
chronology to geological evidence. He distinguished,
however, between facts and theories, and he did not
hesitate to challenge the latter if (like polygenism)
they appeared to contradict essential theological
claims.

When Charles Darwin published his *Origin of
Species*, Hodge objected to the new theory on several
non-theological grounds: among other things, it
offended common sense, it flew in the face of accepted
views of the immutability of species, and it lacked
sufficient evidence. His central objections, however,
were theological.

Of the theological issues which <u>might</u> have provided
grounds for Hodge's critique, biblical chronology was
conspicuously absent. Hodge had already largely
reconciled himself to the modern geological time scale.
Certain other biblical issues were also absent or quite
subordinate: the doctrines of an original human pair,
original perfection, and a historical fall. Hodge
believed in these doctrines, but they had almost
nothing to do with his objection to Darwin's theory.
Critics who imply that Hodge's opposition to Darwinism
was based on biblical fundamentalism are thus
completely mistaken.

To some extent, Hodge objected to Darwinism because
he objected to evolution itself. He believed that the
Bible taught that some kinds of living things were
created directly by God rather than derived from other
forms of life; but he did not confuse these primordial

forms with the species distinguished by modern naturalists, and he was prepared to admit the derivation of at least some of the latter by purely natural forces. Since even Darwin's theory assumed that life was originally breathed by the Creator into a few forms or into one, Hodge's objection on this point might eventually have resolved itself into a dispute over the number and nature of these primordial forms.

A more fundamental basis for Hodge's objection to evolution was his conviction that the emergence of new species required God's providential guidance. Any theory which attributes the origin of species solely to the operation of blind, unintelligent physical causes, -- even if it acknowledges that those physical causes were set in motion by God, -- denies the doctrine of providence, which Hodge considered central to Christian belief. Such a theory, however, need not be atheistic; if it admits an original creative act of God, it could be a form of deism.

Although Hodge suspected that any consistent theory of evolution would tend to be deistic, and therefore theologically unacceptable, he did not rule out the possibility of theistic evolution. Neither the progressive emergence of new species in time, nor the involvement of secondary causes in the process, presented fundamental theological problems for Hodge. He objected to evolution in general only to the extent that it tended to deny God's providential control of the evolutionary process; and it is quite reasonable to suppose that if he had lived long enough he might eventually have converted, like his successors at Princeton Seminary, to some form of theistic evolution.

This is speculation, however, and the fact remains that Hodge was opposed to the notion of evolution in general. This opposition had at least four unfortunate repercussions: it overshadowed those elements in Hodge's theology which could have contributed to a reconciliation between theology and evolutionary biology; it tended, as the scientific evidence for evolution gradually became more convincing, to identify Hodge with opposition to science itself; it added to the already rampant confusion between evolution and Darwinism, even though Hodge had tried so carefully to distinguish the two in his critique; and it obscured his central theological objection to Darwin's particular theory.

His central objection was that Darwin's theory, unlike other theories of evolution, excluded design in living organisms. According to Hodge, Darwinism not only excluded God's providential control of secondary causes, but also ruled out any sort of design in living organisms. Other deistic theories of evolution were at least compatible with a belief that God preprogrammed natural processes to produce specific designed results, but Darwin's proposed mechanism included such a high proportion of chance that designed results seemed unattainable. Darwin's theory was thus unique in being not merely a-teleological, but anti-teleological.

Although Hodge did not necessarily believe that every detail of every living thing was specifically designed by God, he believed that God designed their major features. Above all, Hodge believed that God designed human beings in the divine image, and he objected to Darwinism primarily as a false theory of human origins. He did not, however, object to Darwin's

theory as a threat to the argument _from_ design.
Although Hodge did not formulate it explicitly, he
based his central theological objection to Darwinism on
an argument *to* design:

The Argument To Design

(Modus Tollens Form)

If God exists, then living organisms are
designed.

According to Darwinism, living organisms
are not designed.

Therefore, according to Darwinism God
does not exist.

Hodge thus concluded that Darwinism is tantamount to
atheism.

When Hodge claimed that God's existence entails
design in living organisms, he was representing not
only his own brand of nineteenth-century American
Calvinism, but also the Christian theological tradition
as a whole. For mainstream Christian theology, God's
nature and existence do not necessarily entail the
existence of living things, since God creates by choice
rather than necessity; the question is whether living
organisms, having been created by God, are consequently
designed. Such design is a reasonable inference from
scripture, though of course many Christians would not
interpret scripture as Hodge does. Something like
Hodge's first premise, however, is also found in all
major branches of the Christian theological tradition
up to the nineteenth century, as represented by

Athanasius, Maximus, Augustine, Aquinas, Luther,
Calvin, and Schleiermacher. Although several of these
theologians did not believe that every aspect of living
things must be regarded as designed, they are unanimous
in maintaining that the human species, at least, is
designed or intended by God. This claim is not merely
an opinion which they happen to share; for each of
them, it is a consequence of fundamental Christian
beliefs about God's omnipotence and benevolence, and of
the central doctrine of the incarnation. Furthermore,
the prevalence of this claim in their writings,
compared with two brief references by Aquinas to
teleological proof, indicates that the argument to
design is a much more integral part of Christian
theology than the argument _from_ design.

Although critics have charged Hodge with departing
from the Christian tradition at various points in his
theology, none of their criticisms invalidate his claim
that one consequence of belief in God is a conviction
that human beings, at least, are designed. The first
premise of Hodge's argument is thus representative of
mainstream Christianity, at least up through the
nineteenth century.

The second premise of Hodge's argument is that
Darwinism denies design. Nineteenth-century Darwinians
disagreed over the implications of Darwin's theory for
design. Darwin himself believed that the theory might
be compatible with a general notion of designed laws,
but he was convinced that it excluded design in any
particular result of evolution, such as the human
species. Huxley saw Darwinism as the death-blow to
coarser forms of teleology, and spoke of a wider
teleology; but he interpreted the theory in a

deterministic sense which implied that either
everything in nature is designed, or nothing is, and he
seems personally to have opted for the latter. Gray
and Wright reconstructed the argument from design to
accommodate Darwin's notion of designed laws; but in
addition they continued to read more detailed design
into the theory, despite Darwin's objection that it was
illogical. There was thus no unanimity among the
Darwinians on the issue of design.

There are, however, good reasons for choosing
Darwin's view as the normative interpretation: he was
more committed to the theory and less committed to
design than Gray and Wright, and thus more likely to
consider the issue dispassionately; he gave the issue
more thought than Huxley; and his interpretation is a
reasoned deduction from the two main elements of the
theory, variation and natural selection.

In Darwin's interpretation, there is no way that
his theory could lead to designed results in any
particular product of the evolutionary process. The
human species, as the latest in a long line of such
results, is a fortiori undesigned. Although some
versions of the argument to design maintain (like
Darwinism) that some details are left to chance, they
all insist that the human species is not one of those
details. Since the argument to design concludes that
the very nature and existence of God entails design in
the human species, Darwin's interpretation of Darwinism
is thus tantamount to atheism. The possible
compatibility of Darwin's theory with a general notion
that God designed the order of the universe does not
help matters: if the details are left to chance, and

one of those details is the human species, the logical force of Hodge's critique is undiminished.

What are the implications of this conclusion? Of the many participants in the nineteenth-century Darwinian controversies, only a few have been dealt with in this study; and of the many social factors and intellectual issues involved, only one has been examined in detail. Obviously, a single conclusion based on such a small sample cannot adequately characterize the controversies as a whole. On the other hand, in nineteenth-century America Charles Hodge was the most prominent theological opponent of Darwinism, and design the most prominent theological issue, at least among educated people. Therefore, the conclusion that Hodge's opposition was based on the argument _to_ design has several important implications.

First, it challenges the received view that the most serious theological opposition to Darwinism was based on the argument _from_ design. It is undoubtedly true that some people opposed Darwinism because they were committed to the argument _from_ design, and that at least one proponent of the argument _to_ design (Newman) counselled reconciliation. Nevertheless, because of his prominence Hodge represents a major counter-example to the received view, which clearly needs to be re-evaluated.

Second, the conclusion of this study challenges the perception that a major nineteenth-century objection to Darwinism was unrepresentative of the Christian tradition as a whole. Since the argument from design played a relatively minor role in Christian theology until it rose to prominence in Britain and America in the eighteenth and nineteenth centuries, the received view suggests that the major basis for theological opposition to Darwinism was a historical anomaly. The argument to design, however, was a much more integral part of the Christian tradition than the argument from design. This helps to explain why Hume and Kant aroused less widespread religious concern than Darwin: what the former attacked was theologically dispensable, but what the latter attacked was theologically essential. It also means that Christian opposition to Darwinism cannot be so easily relegated to the backwaters of history or to backwoods fundamentalism: as some recent studies have suggested, the theological conflict may not yet be resolved.

It is important to remember that the conflict described here is not between the Bible and evolution: it is between the Christian theological tradition, up to and including Schleiermacher, and Darwin's theory that evolution is caused by the natural selection of accidental variations. Charles Hodge and Charles Darwin were both convinced that the two are logically irreconcilable: a person may consistently believe in either Christianity or Darwinism, but not both.

There are, of course, many people who disagree, and who regard Christianity and Darwinism as perfectly compatible with each other. The two cannot be regarded as compatible, however, unless the former is taken to mean something other than what the mainstream theological tradition has meant by Christianity, or the latter is taken to mean something other than what Charles Darwin meant by Darwinism.

BIBLIOGRAPHY

Adler, Mortimer J. *Problems for Thomists: The Problem of Species*. New York: Sheed & Ward, 1940.

Ahlstrom, Sydney E. "The Scottish Philosophy and American Theology." *Church History* 24 (1955): 257-272.

_____. "Theology in America: A Historical Survey." In *The Shaping of American Religion*, edited by James Ward Smith and A. Leland Jamison. Princeton: Princeton University Press, 1961.

Aldrich, Michele L. "United States: Bibliographical Essay." In *The Comparative Reception of Darwinism*, edited by Thomas F. Glick. Austin: University of Texas Press, 1974.

Althaus, Paul. "Der Schöpfungsgedanke bei Luther." *Sitzungsberichte der bayerischen Akademie der Wissenschaften* 7 (1959): 1-18.

_____. *The Theology of Martin Luther*. Translated by Robert C. Schultz. Philadelphia: Fortress Press, 1966.

"American Lights of the Evangelical Alliance." *Sunday School Times* (October 18, 1873). Handwritten excerpt. Charles A. Hodge Letters and Papers. Princeton University Library, Princeton University, Princeton, New Jersey.

Anderson, F.H. *The Philosophy of Francis Bacon*. Chicago: University of Chicago Press, 1948.

Aquinas, Thomas. *Commentary on the Gospel of St. John*. Edited by James A. Weisheipl and Fabian R. Larcher. Aquinas Scripture Series, vol.4. Albany, New York: Magi Books, 1980.

226

Aquinas, Thomas. *On the Power of God*. Translated by the English Dominican Fathers. First Book, Questions 1-111. Westminster, Maryland: Newman Press, 1952.

_____. *Summa Contra Gentiles*. Book 1. Translated by Anton C. Pegis. London: Notre Dame Press, 1955.

_____. *Summa Contra Gentiles*. Book 2. Translated by James F. Anderson. London: Notre Dame Press, 1956.

_____. *Summa Theologica*. Translated by Fathers of the English Dominican Province. 3 vols. New York: Benziger Brothers, 1947.

_____. *Truth*. Translated by Robert W. Mulligan. Vol. 1, Questions 1-9. Chicago: Henry Regnery, 1952.

Athanasius. *Select Works and Letters*. Edited by Philip Schaff. A Select Library of the Nicene and Post-Nicene Fathers of the Christian Church, 2d Series, vol. 7. Grand Rapids, Michigan: Wm. B. Eerdmans, 1974.

Augustine. *Earlier Writings*. Translated by John H. S. Burleigh. The Library of Christian Classics, vol. 4. Philadelphia: Westminster Press, n.d.

_____. *Eighty-Three Different Questions*. Translated by David Mosher. Washington, D.C.: Catholic University of America Press, 1982.

_____. *Homilies on the Gospel of John*. Edited by Philip Schaff. A Select Library of the Nicene and Post-Nicene Fathers of the Christian Church, vol. 7. Grand Rapids, Michigan: Wm. B. Eerdmans, 1974.

_____. *Letters*. Translated by Wilfred Parsons. Vol. 1, Letters 1-82. Washington, D.C.: Catholic University of America Press, 1951.

_____. *The Literal Meaning of Genesis*. Translated by John Hammond Taylor. Vol. 1, Books 1-6. Ancient Christian Writers, no. 41. New York: Newman Press, 1982.

_____. *On the Holy Trinity, Doctrinal Treatises, Moral Treatises*. Edited by Philip Schaff. A Select Library of the Nicene and Post-Nicene Fathers of the Christian Church, vol. 3. Grand Rapids, Michigan: Wm. B. Eerdmans, 1974.

Augustine. *The Teacher, The Free Choice of the Will, Grace and Free Will*. Translated by Robert P. Russell. Washington,D.C.: Catholic University of America Press, 1968.

_____. *The Writings Against the Manichaeans and Against the Donatists*. Edited by Philip Schaff. A Select Library of the Nicene and Post-Nicene Fathers of the Christian Church, vol. 4. Grand Rapids, Michigan: Wm. B. Eerdmans, 1974.

Bacon, Francis. *The Works of Francis Bacon*. Edited by James Spedding, Robert Leslie Ellis, and Douglas Denon Heath. 1870. Reprint. New York: Garret Press, 1968.

Baker, George. Notes of Charles Hodge's Theology Lectures at Princeton Theological Seminary, 1861-1862. Presbyterian Historical Society, Philadelphia, Pennsylvania.

Balmer, Randall H. "The Princetonians and Scripture: A Reconsideration." *Westminster Theological Journal* 44 (1982): 352-365.

Barth, Karl. *Protestant Theology in the Nineteenth Century*. Valley Forge, Pennsylvania: Judson Press, 1973.

Barzun, Jaques. *Darwin, Marx, Wagner*. 1941. Reprint. Garden City, New York: Doubleday & Company, 1958.

Basil. *Letters and Select Works*. Edited by Philip Schaff and Henry Wace. A Select Library of the Nicene and Post-Nicene Fathers of the Christian Church, 2d series, vol.8. Grand Rapids, Michigan: Wm. B. Eerdmans, 1975.

Beardslee, John Walter III. "Theological Development at Geneva Under Francis and Jean-Alphonse Turretin." Ph.D. diss., Yale University, 1956.

Berg, Kenneth P. "Charles A. Hodge, Controversialist." Ph.D. diss., University of Iowa, 1952.

Borome, Joseph A. "The Evolution Controversy." In *Essays in American Historiography*, edited by Donald Sheehan and Harold C. Syrett. New York: Columbia University Press, 1960.

Bowler, Peter J. "Darwinism and the Argument from Design: Suggestions for a Reevaluation." *Journal of the History of Biology* 10 (1977): 29-43.

Bowler, Peter J. *Evolution: The History of an Idea.* Berkeley: University of California Press, 1984.

Bozeman, Theodore Dwight. *Protestants in an Age of Science.* Chapel Hill: University of North Carolina Press, 1977.

Brandt, Richard B. *The Philosophy of Schleiermacher.* New York: Harper & Brothers, 1941.

Calvin, John. *Commentary upon the Acts of the Apostles.* 2 vols. Translated by Henry Beveridge. Grand Rapids, Michigan: Wm B. Eerdmans, 1949.

_____. *Commentary on the Book of Psalms.* 5 vols. Translated by James Anderson. Grand Rapids, Michigan: Wm B. Eerdmans, 1949.

_____. *Commentaries on the Epistle to the Hebrews.* Translated by John Owen. Grand Rapids, Michigan: Wm B. Eerdmans, 1949.

_____. *Commentary on the First Book of Moses Called Genesis.* 2 vols. Translated by John King. Grand Rapids, Michigan: Wm B. Eerdmans, 1948.

_____. *Commentary on the Gospel According to John.* 2 vols. Translated by William Pringle. Grand Rapids, Michigan: Wm B. Eerdmans, 1956.

_____. *Institutes of the Christian Religion.* 2 vols. Edited by John T. McNeill. Library of Christian Classics. Philadelphia: Westminster Press, 1960.

Clark, Joseph. "The Scepticism of Science." *The Biblical Repertory and Princeton Review* 35 (1863): 43-75.

Copleston, F.C. *Aquinas.* Harmondsworth, Middlesex: Penguin, 1955.

_____. *A History of Philosophy.* Revised edition. 8 vols. Garden City, New York: Doubleday, 1962.

Cupitt, Don. "Darwinism and English Religious Thought." *Theology* 78 (1975): 125-131.

Dabney, Robert L. "Hodge's Systematic Theology." *The Southern Presbyterian Review* 24 (1873): 167-225.

Danhof, Ralph J. *Charles Hodge as a Dogmatician*. Goes, The Netherlands: Oosternaan & Le Cointre, 1929.

Daniels, George H. *American Science in the Age of Jackson*. New York: Columbia University Press, 1968.

_____, ed. *Darwinism Comes to America*. Waltham, Massachusetts: Blaisdell, 1968.

D'Arcy, M. C. "The Philosophy of St. Augustine." In *Saint Augustine*, edited by M. C. D'Arcy. Cleveland: World, 1957.

Darwin, Charles. *The Descent of Man and Selection in Relation to Sex*. 2 vols. New York: D. Appleton, 1871.

_____. *On the Origin of Species by Means of Natural Selection: or the Preservation of Favoured Races in the Struggle for Life*. 5th edition. London: John Murray, 1869.

_____. *The Variation of Plants and Animals Under Domestication*. 2 vols. New York: Orange Judd, 1868.

Darwin, Francis, ed. *The Life and Letters of Charles Darwin*. 2 vols. New York: D. Appleton, 1887.

Darwin, Francis, and A. C. Seward, eds. *More Letters of Charles Darwin*. 2 vols. New York: D. Appleton, 1903.

Davis, Dennis Royal. "Presbyterian Attitudes Toward Science and the Coming of Darwinism in America, 1859-1929." Ph.D. diss., University of Illinois, 1980.

de Beer, Gavin. *Charles Darwin: Evolution by Natural Selection*. 1963. Reprint. Westport, Connecticut: Greenwood Press, 1976.

Dillenberger, John. *Protestant Thought and Natural Science*. Garden City: Doubleday, 1960.

_____, ed. *Martin Luther: Selections from His Writings*. Garden City, New York: Doubleday, 1961.

Dowey, Edward A., Jr. *The Knowledge of God in Calvin's Theology*. New York: Columbia University Press, 1952.

Draper, John William. *History of the Conflict between Religion and Science.* 17th edition. London: Kegan Paul, Trench & Co., 1883.

Dupré, Louis. *A Dubious Heritage.* New York: Paulist Press, 1977.

Dupree, A. Hunter. *Asa Gray, 1810-1888.* Cambridge, Massachusetts: Harvard University Press, 1959.

Ebeling, Gerhard. "Schleiermacher's Doctrine of the Divine Attributes." In *Schleiermacher as Contemporary,* edited by Robert W. Funk. Journal for Theology and the Church, no. 7. New York: Herder & Herder, 1970.

Eckard, James R. "The Logical Relations of Religion and Natural Science." *The Biblical Repertory and Princeton Review* 32 (1860): 574-608.

Eiseley, Loren. *Darwin's Century.* Garden City, New York: Doubleday, 1961.

Ellegard, Alvar. *Darwin and the General Reader: The Reception of Darwin's Theory of Evolution in the British Periodical Press, 1859-1872.* Goteborg: Universitets Arsskrift, 1958.

_____. "The Darwinian Theory and the Argument from Design." *Lychnos* (1956): 173-192.

_____. "The Darwinian Theory and Nineteenth-Century Philosophies of Science." *Journal of the History of Ideas* 18 (1957): 362-393.

Encyclopedia of Religion and Ethics. Edited by James Hastings. Vol. 3. New York: Charles Scribner's Sons, 1928.

Farnham, [?]. Notes of Charles Hodge's Theology Lectures at Princeton Theological Seminary, 1857. Charles A. Hodge Papers. Speer Library, Princeton Theological Seminary, Princeton, New Jersey.

Florovsky, George. *Collected Works of George Florovsky.* 4 vols. to date. Belmont, Massachusetts: Nordland, 1976.

_____. "The Idea of Creation in Christian Philosophy." *Eastern Churches Quarterly* 8 (1949-1950): 53-77.

Foster, Frank Hugh. *The Modern Movement in American Theology*. New York: Fleming H. Revell, 1939.

Garrigou-Lagrange, Reginald. *The Trinity and the Creator: A Commentary on St. Thomas' Theological Summa, 1a, qq. 27-119*. St. Louis, Missouri: B. Herder, 1952.

Geiger, L. B. "Les Idées Divines dans l'Oeuvre de S. Thomas." In *Saint Thomas Aquinas 1274-1974: Commemorative Studies*. Vol. 1. Toronto: Pontifical Institute of Mediaeval Studies, 1974.

Gerrish, B.A. *A Prince of the Church: Schleiermacher and the Beginnings of Modern Theology*. Philadelphia: Fortress Press, 1984.

Ghiselin, Michael T. *The Triumph of the Darwinian Method*. Berkeley: University of California Press, 1969.

Gillespie, Neal C. *Charles Darwin and the Problem of Creation*. Chicago: University of Chicago Press, 1979.

Gillispie, Charles Coulston. *Genesis and Geology*. 1951. Reprint. New York: Harper & Row, 1959.

Gilson, Etienne. *The Christian Philosophy of Saint Augustine*. Translated by L. E. M. Lynch. New York: Random House, 1960.

_____. *The Christian Philosophy of St. Thomas Aquinas*. Translated by L.K. Shook. New York: Random House, 1956.

Goodman, Lenn E. and Madeleine J. Goodman. "Creation and Evolution: Another Round in an Ancient Struggle." *Zygon* 18, no.1 (March, 1983): 3-43.

Grave, S.A. *The Scottish Philosophy of Common Sense*. Oxford: Clarendon Press, 1960.

Gray, Asa. "Charles Robert Darwin." *Nature* 10 (1874): 79-81.

_____. *Darwiniana*. New York: D. Appleton, 1876.

_____. *Natural Science and Religion*. New York: Charles Scribner's Sons, 1880.

_____. "Variation of Animals and Plants Under Domestication." *The Nation* 6 (March 19, 1868): 234-236.

Gray, Jane Loring, ed. *Letters of Asa Gray.* 2 vols. New York: Burt Franklin, 1973.

Greene, John C. *Darwin and the Modern World View.* Baton Rouge, Louisiana: Louisiana State University Press, 1961.

_____. *The Death of Adam.* Ames, Iowa: University of Iowa Press, 1959.

Gruber, Howard E. *Darwin on Man.* 1974. Reprint. Chicago: University of Chicago Press, 1981.

Harlow, Henry. Notes of Charles Hodge's Theology Lectures at Princeton Theological Seminary, 1856-1857. Charles A. Hodge Papers. Speer Library, Princeton Theological Seminary, Princeton, New Jersey.

Henle, R.J. *Saint Thomas and Platonism.* The Hague: Martinus Nijhoff, 1956.

Himmelfarb, Gertrude. *Darwin and the Darwinian Revolution.* 1959. Reprint. New York: W.W. Norton, 1968.

Hodge, Archibald A. *The Life of Charles Hodge D.D. LL.D.* New York: Charles Scribner's Sons, 1880.Hodge, Casper W. and Classmate. Notes of Charles Hodge's Theology Lectures at Princeton Theological Seminary, 1852-1853. Charles A. Hodge Papers. Speer Library, Princeton Theological Seminary, Princeton, New Jersey.

Hodge, Charles A. "Address." In *Proceedings Connected with the Semi-Centennial Commemoration of the Professorship Rev. Charles Hodge, D.D., LL.D. in the Theological Seminary at Princeton, N.J., April 24, 1872.* New York: Anson D.F. Randolph, 1872.

_____. "The Bible in Science." *New York Observer* (March 26, 1863): 98-99.

_____. "Diversity of Species in the Human Race." *The Biblical Repertory and Princeton Review* 34 (1862): 435-464.

_____. "The First and Second Adam." *The Biblical Repertory and Princeton Review* 32 (1860): 335-376.

_____. Lecture Notes on "Creation." [1840's ?] Charles A. Hodge Papers. Speer Library, Princeton Theological Seminary, Princeton, New Jersey.

Hodge, Charles A. "Polemic Theology." Charles A. Hodge Papers. Speer Library, Princeton Theological Seminary, Princeton, Jersey.

_____. *Systematic Theology*. 3 vols. 1871-1873. Reprint. Grand Rapids, Michigan: Wm. B. Eerdmans, 1981.

_____. "The Unity of Mankind." *The Biblical Repertory and Princeton Review* 31 (1859): 103-149.

_____. *What is Darwinism?*. New York: Scribner, Armstrong, & Co., 1874.

Hoffecker, W. Andrew. *Piety and the Princeton Theologians*. Phillipsburg, New Jersey: Presbyterian and Reformed Publishing Co., 1981.

Hofstadter, Richard, and Walter P. Metzger. *The Development of Academic Freedom in The United States*. New York: Columbia University Press, 1955.

Holifield, E. Brooks. *The Gentlemen Theologians*. Durham, North Carolina: Duke University Press, 1978.

Hooykaas, R. *Religion and the Rise of Modern Science*. Edinburgh: Scottish Academic Press, 1972.

Hope, M.B. "On the Relation between the Holy Scriptures and some parts of Geological Science." *The Biblical Repertory and Princeton Review* 13 (1841): 368-394.

Hovenkamp, Herbert. *Science and Religion in America, 1800-1860*. Philadelphia: University of Pennsylvania Press, 1978.

Hull, David L. *Darwin and His Critics*. 1973. Reprint. Chicago: University of Chicago Press, 1983.

Hume, David. *Dialogues Concerning Natural Religion*. Edited by Norman Kemp Smith. Indianapolis: Bobbs-Merrill, 1947.

Hurlbutt, Robert H., III. *Hume, Newton, and the Design Argument*. Lincoln, Nebraska: University of Nebraska Press, 1965.

Huxley, Thomas Henry. *Collected Essays*. 9 vols. London: Macmillan, 1893-1894.

234

Huxley, Leonard. *Life and Letters of Thomas Henry Huxley*.
    3 vols. London: Macmillan, 1913.

Illick, Joseph E. "The Reception of Darwinism at the
    Theological Seminary and the College at Princeton, New
    Jersey." *Journal of the Presbyterian Historical Society*
    38 (1960): 152-165, 234-243.

Irvine, William. *Apes, Angels, and Victorians*. New York:
    McGraw-Hill, 1955.

Johnson, Deryl Freeman. "The Attitudes of the Princeton
    Theologians Toward Darwinism and Evolution from 1859-
    1929." Ph.D. diss., University of Iowa, 1968.

Kant, Immanuel. *Critique of Pure Reason*. Translated by
    Norman Kemp Smith. New York: St. Martin's Press, 1965.

_____. *Prolegomena to Any Future Metaphysics*. Translated
    by Peter G. Lucas. Manchester: Manchester University
    Press, 1953.

Kelly, J.N.D. *Early Christian Doctrines*. Revised
    edition. San Francisco: Harper & Row, 1978.

Kelsey, David H. *The Uses of Scripture in Recent Theology*.
    Philadelphia: Fortress Press, 1975.

Klaaren, Eugene M. *Religious Origins of Modern Science*.
    Grand Rapids, Michigan: Wm. B. Eerdmans, 1977.

Lack, David. *Evolutionary Theory and Christian Belief: The
    Unresolved Conflict*. London: Methuen, 1957.

Lehrer, Keith and Ronald E. Beanblossom, eds. *Thomas
    Reid's Inquiry and Essays*. Indianapolis: Bobbs-Merrill,
    1975.

Leith, John H. *Creeds of the Churches*. 1963. Reprint.
    Atlanta: John Knox Press, 1977.

Lindsay, Thomas M. "The Doctrine of Scripture." *The
    Expositor*, 5th Series 1 (1895): 278-293.

Livingston, James C. "Darwin, Darwinism, and Theology:
    Recent Studies." *Religious Studies Review* 8 (April,
    1982): 105-115.

Livingstone, David N. "The Idea of Design: The Vicissitudes of a Key Concept in the Princeton Response to Darwin." *Scottish Journal of Theology* 37 (1984): 329-357.

Loetscher, Lefferts A. *The Broadening Church.* Philadephia: University of Pennsylvania Press, 1954.

Loewenberg, Bert James. "The Controversy Over Evolution in New England, 1859-1873." *New England Quarterly* 8 (1935): 232-257.

_____. "The Impact of the Doctrine of Evolution on American Thought." Ph.D. diss., Harvard University, 1934.

Lofgren, David. *Die Theologie der Schöpfung bei Luther.* Göttingen: Vandenhoeck & Ruprecht, 1960.

Luther, Martin. *Luther's Works.* Edited by Jaroslav Pelikan (vols. 1-30) and Helmut Lehman (vols. 31-55). 55 vols. St. Louis, Missouri: Concordia, 1958.

McAllister, James L., Jr. "The Nature of Religious Knowledge in the Theology of Charles Hodge." Ph.D. diss., Duke University, 1957.

McCosh, James. *The Scottish Philosophy.* 1874. Reprint. Hildesheim, Germany: Georg Olms Buchhandlung, 1966.

McGiffert, Michael. "Christian Darwinism: The Partnership of Asa Gray and George Frederick Wright, 1874-1881." Ph.D. diss., Yale University, 1958.

MacGregor, James. "Dr. Charles Hodge and the Princeton School." *The British and Foreign Evangelical Review* 23 (1874): 456-469.

McInerny, Ralph. *St. Thomas Aquinas.* Notre Dame: University of Notre Dame Press, 1982.

McKeough, Michael J. "The Meaning of the Rationes Seminales in St. Augustine." Ph.D. diss., Catholic University of America, 1926.

McPherson, Thomas. *The Argument from Design.* London: Macmillan, 1972.

Mandelbaum, Maurice. "Darwin's Religious Views." *Journal of the History of Ideas* 19 (1958): 363-378.

Manier, Edward. *The Young Darwin and His Cultural Circle.* Dordrecht, Holland: D. Reidel, 1978.

Marsden, George M. "Creation Versus Evolution: No Middle Way." *Nature* 305 (1983): 571-574.

_____. Fundamentalism and American Culture. New York: Oxford University Press, 1980.

Maximus. *The Ascetic Life. The Four Centuries on Charity.* Translated by Polycarp Sherwood. Ancient Christian Writers, vol. 21. Westminster, Maryland: Longmans, Green & Co., 1955.

Meijering, E.P. *Orthodoxy and Platonism in Athanasius: Synthesis or Antithesis?.* Leiden: E.J. Brill, 1974.

Meyendorff, John. *Byzantine Theology: Historical Trends and Doctrinal Themes.* New York: Fordham University Press, 1974.

_____. *Christ in Near Eastern Thought.* Washington, D.C.: Corpus Books, 1969.

Millhauser, Milton. "The Scriptural Geologists." *Osiris* 11 (1954): 65-86.

Moore, James R. "Creation and the Problem of Charles Darwin." *British Journal for the History of Science* 14 (1981): 189-200.

_____. *The Post-Darwinian Controversies.* Cambridge: Cambridge University Press, 1979.

Nelson, John Oliver. "The Rise of the Princeton Theology." Ph.D. diss., Yale University, 1935.

New Catholic Encyclopedia. Vol. 9. New York: McGraw-Hill, 1967.

Newman, John Henry. *Letters and Diaries.* Edited by Charles S. Dessain and Thomas Gornall. Vol. 25. Oxford: Clarendon Press, 1973.

Niebuhr, Richard R. "Schleiermacher and the Names of God." *In Schleiermacher as Contemporary*, edited by Robert W. Funk. Journal for Theology and the Church, no. 7. New York: Herder & Herder, 1970.

_____. *Schleiermacher on Christ and Religion*. New York: Charles Scribner's Sons, 1964.

Niesel, Wilhelm. *The Theology of Calvin*. Translated by Harold Knight. Philadelphia: Westminster Press, 1956.

Noll, Mark A., ed. *The Princeton Theology, 1812-1912*. Grand Rapids, Michigan: Baker Book House, 1983.

Numbers, Ronald L. "Science and Religion." *Osiris*, 2nd series 1 (1985): 59-80.

O'Grady, Richard T. "Evolutionary Theory and Teleology." *Journal of Theoretical Biology* 107 (1984): 563-578.

Origen. "De Principiis." In *Tertullian; Minucius Felix; Commodian; Origen*, edited by Alexander Roberts and James Donaldson. The Ante-Nicene Fathers, vol.4. Grand Rapids, Michigan: Wm. B. Eerdmans, 1972.

Ospovat, Dov. *The Development of Darwin's Theory*. Cambridge: Cambridge University Press, 1981.

_____. "God and Natural Selection: The Darwinian Idea of Design." *Journal of the History of Biology* 13 (1980): 169-194.

O'Toole, Christopher. *The Philosophy of Creation in the Writings of St. Augustine*. Washington, D.C.: Catholic University of America Press, 1944.

Paley, William. *Natural Theology*. 1802. Reprint. Houston: St. Thomas Press, 1972.

Parkinson, George H. "Charles Darwin's Influence on Religion and Politics of the Present Day." Ph.D. diss., University of Chicago, 1942.

Patton, Francis. "Charles Hodge." *The Presbyterian Review* 2 (1881): 348-377.

238

Pauck, Wilhelm. "Schleiermacher's Conception of History
    and Church History." *In Schleiermacher as Contemporary*,
    edited by Robert W. Funk. Journal for Theology and the
    Church, no. 7. New York: Herder & Herder, 1970.

Peckham, Morse. *The Triumph of Romanticism*. Columbia,
    South Carolina: University of South Carolina Press, 1970.

Pelikan, Jaroslav. *The Christian Tradition*. 4 vols. to
    date. Chicago: University of Chicago Press, 1971-.

Persons, Stow., ed. *Evolutionary Thought in America*.
    1950. Reprint. Hamden, Connecticut: Archon Books, 1968.

Pfeifer, Edward Justin. "The Reception of Darwinism in the
    United States, 1859-1880." Ph.D. diss., Brown
    University, 1957.

_____. "United States." In *The Comparative Reception of
    Darwinism,* edited by Thomas F. Glick. Austin: University
    of Texas Press, 1974.

Portalie, Eugene. *A Guide to the Thought of Saint
    Augustine*. Translated by Ralph J. Bastian. Westport,
    Connecticut: Greenwood Press, 1975.

Prenter, Regin. *Spiritus Creator*. Translated by John M.
    Jensen. Philadelphia: Muhlenberg Press, 1953.

Quasten, Johannes. *Patrology*. 3 vols. Utrecht: Spectrum,
    1966.

Redeker, Martin. *Schleiermacher: Life and Thought*.
    Translated by John Wallhausser. Philadephia: Fortress
    Press, 1973.

Rogers, Jack B., and Donald K. McKim. *The Authority and
    Interpretation of the Bible*. San Francisco: Harper &
    Row, 1979.

Ruse, Michael. *The Darwinian Revolution*. Chicago:
    University of Chicago Press, 1979.

Russell, E. S. *Form and Function*. 1916. Reprint.
    Chicago: University of Chicago Press, 1982.

Russett, Cynthia Eagle. *Darwin in America: The
    Intellectual Response,* 1865-1912. San Francisco: W.H.
    Freeman, 1976.

Sandeen, Ernest R. "The Princeton Theology." *Church History* 31 (1962): 307-321.

_____. *The Roots of Fundamentalism*. Chicago: University of Chicago Press, 1970.

Schaff, Philip. *The Creeds of Christendom*. 3 vols. 1877. Reprint. Grand Rapids, Michigan: Baker Book House, 1969.

_____. *Theological Propaedeutic*. New York: Scribners, 1898.

Schaff, Philip and S. Irenaeus Prime, eds. *History, Essays, Orations, and other Documents of the Sixth General Conference of the Evangelical Alliance, Held in New York, October 2-12, 1873*. New York: Harper & Brothers, 1874.

Schleiermacher, Friedrich. *The Christian Faith*. 2d edition. Edited by H.R. Mackintosh and J.S. Stewart. Philadelphia: Fortress Press, 1928.

_____. *On the Glaubenslehre: Two Letters to Dr. Lucke*. Translated by James Duke and Francis Fiorenza. Chico, California: Scholars Press, 1981.

_____. *On Religion: Speeches to its Cultured Despisers*. Translated by John Oman. New York: Harper & Row, 1958.

"Scripture and Science." *New York Observer* (March 12, 1863): 82.

Sherwood, Polycarp. *The Earlier Ambigua of Saint Maximus the Confessor and His Refutation of Origenism*. Studia Anselmiana, no. 36. Rome: Orbis Catholicus/Herder, 1955.

"Short Notices." *The Biblical Repertory and Princeton Review* 23 (1851): 554-557.

"Short Notices." *The Biblical Repertory and Princeton Review* 23 (1851): 696-699.

"Short Notices." *The Biblical Repertory and Princeton Review* 28 (1856): 161-163.

Sloan, Douglas. *The Scottish Enlightenment and the American College Ideal*. New York: Columbia Teachers College Press, 1971.

Smith, Gary S. "Calvinists and Evolution, 1870-1920." *Journal of Presbyterian History* 61 (1983): 335-352.

Smith, Norman Kemp. *A Commentary to Kant's "Critique of Pure Reason"*. 2d edition, revised. Portway, Bath: Cedric Chivers, 1969.

Stewart, Dugald. *Philosophical Essays*. Edinburgh: George Ramsey, 1810.

Student's Notes of Charles Hodge's Theology Lectures at Princeton Theological Seminary, 1842-1843. Charles A. Hodge Papers. Speer Library, Princeton Theological Seminary, Princeton, New Jersey.

TeSelle, Eugene. *Augustine the Theologian*. New York: Herder and Herder, 1970.

Thiel, John E. *God and World in Schleiermacher's Dialektik and Glaubenslehre*. Bern: Peter Lang, 1981.

Thunberg, Lars. *Microcosm and Mediator*. Copenhagen: C.W.K. Gleerup Lund, 1965

Tsirpanlis, Constantine N. "Aspects of Maximian Theology of Politics, History, and the Kingdom of God." *The Patristic & Byzantine Review* 1 (1981): 1-21.

_____. "Aspects of Athanasian Soteriology." In *Greek Patristic Theology*. Monograph Series in Orthodox Theology, no. 3. New York: Eo Press, 1979.

Torrance, T. F. *Calvin's Doctrine of Man*. London: Lutterworth Press, 1949.

Turner, Frank M. *Between Science and Religion: The Reaction to Scientific Naturalism in Late Victorian England*. New Haven: Yale University Press, 1974.

_____. "The Victorian Conflict between Science and Religion: A Professional Dimension." *Isis* 69 (1978): 356-376.

Turretin, Francis. *Institutio Theologiae Elencticae*. Partial handwritten translation by George M. Giger. Charles A. Hodge Papers. Speer Library, Princeton Theological Seminary, Princeton, New Jersey.

Vander Stelt, John C. *Philosophy and Scripture*. Marlton, New Jersey: Mack, 1978.

Wallace, Ronald S. *Calvin's Doctrine of the Word and Sacrament*. 1953. Reprint. Tyler, Texas: Geneva Divinity School Press, 1982.

Watson, Philip S. *Let God Be God: An Interpretation of the Theology of Martin Luther*. London: Epworth Press, 1947.

Welch, Claude. *Protestant Thought in the Nineteenth Century*. 2 vols. New Haven: Yale University Press, 1972 and 1985.

Wells. David. "The Stout and Persistent 'Theology' of Charles Hodge." *Christianity Today* 18 (1974): 1278.

Wendel, François. *Calvin*. Translated by Philip Mairet. London: Collins, 1963.

White, Andrew Dickson. *A History of the Warfare of Science with Theology*. 2 vols. New York: D. Appleton, 1896.

White, Edward A. *Science and Religion in American Thought*. Stanford, California: Stanford University Press, 1952.

Williams, Robert R. *Schleiermacher the Theologian*. Philadelphia: Fortress Press, 1978.

Wilson, David B. "Darwin and the Protestants." *British Journal for the History of Science* 14 (1981): 200-202.

Wolfson, Harry Austryn. *The Philosophy of the Church Fathers*. 3rd edition, revised. Cambridge, Massachusetts: Harvard University Press, 1970.

Woodbridge, John D. "Does the Bible Teach Science?" *Bibliotheca Sacra* 142 (July-Sep 1985): 195-209.

Woodfield, Andrew. *Teleology*. Cambridge: Cambridge University Press, 1976.

Wright, George Frederick. "Concerning the True Doctrine of Final Cause or Design in Nature." *Bibliotheca Sacra* 34 (1877): 355-385.

_____. "The Debt of the Church to Asa Gray." *Bibliotheca Sacra* 45 (1888): 523-530.

242

Wright, George Frederick. "The Divine Method of Producing Living Species." *Bibliotheca Sacra* 33 (1876): 448-493.

_____. "The Evolutionary Fad." *Bibliotheca Sacra* 57 (1900): 303-316.

_____. "Objections to Darwinism, and the Rejoinders of its Advocates." *Bibliotheca Sacra* 33 (1876): 656-694.

_____. *Scientific Aspects of Christian Evidences*. New York: D. Appleton, 1898.

_____. "Some Analogies Between Calvinism and Darwinism." *Bibliotheca Sacra* 37 (1880): 48-76.

Young, Robert M. *Darwin's Metaphor*. Cambridge: Cambridge University Press: 1985.

INDEX

STUDIES IN AMERICAN RELIGION